Acknowledgments

First, I'd like to thank Sruthi Kutty for approaching me about the idea of writing an introductory book about Qt Creator. Second, I'd like to thank Sageer Parkar for shepherding the project throughout the process at Packt, making my first experience with Packt Publishing a painless one. I was fortunate to have several technical reviewers and editors on the project who gave their time graciously to improve the book. Finally, I'd like to thank my wife and son for their patience with me as I undertook yet another book.

About the Reviewers

Lee Zhi Eng is a 3D artist-turned-programmer who worked as a game artist and game programmer in several local game studios in his country, before becoming a contractor and a part time lecturer at a local university, teaching game development subjects, particularly related to Unity Engine and Unreal Development Kit. You can find more information about him at `http://www.zhieng.com`.

Niels Holst graduated from the University of Copenhagen, Denmark with a PhD in Biology. He currently works at Aarhus University, Denmark where he applies Computer Science to solve problems in Applied Ecology. He is a leader of the Universal Simulator open source project.

Application Development with Qt Creator

A fast-paced guide for building cross-platform applications using Qt and Qt Quick

Ray Rischpater

BIRMINGHAM - MUMBAI

Application Development with Qt Creator

Copyright © 2013 Packt Publishing

All rights reserved. No part of this book may be reproduced, stored in a retrieval system, or transmitted in any form or by any means, without the prior written permission of the publisher, except in the case of brief quotations embedded in critical articles or reviews.

Every effort has been made in the preparation of this book to ensure the accuracy of the information presented. However, the information contained in this book is sold without warranty, either express or implied. Neither the author, nor Packt Publishing, and its dealers and distributors will be held liable for any damages caused or alleged to be caused directly or indirectly by this book.

Packt Publishing has endeavored to provide trademark information about all of the companies and products mentioned in this book by the appropriate use of capitals. However, Packt Publishing cannot guarantee the accuracy of this information.

First published: November 2013

Production Reference: 1131113

Published by Packt Publishing Ltd.
Livery Place
35 Livery Street
Birmingham B3 2PB, UK.

ISBN 978-1-78328-231-9

www.packtpub.com

Cover Image by Siddhart Ravishankar (sidd.ravishankar@gmail.com)

Credits

Author
Ray Rischpater

Reviewers
Lee Zhi Eng
Niels Holst
Kamakshi Subramaniam

Acquisition Editors
Vinay Argekar
Aarti Kumaraswamy

Commissioning Editor
Sruthi Kutty

Technical Editors
Hardik B. Soni
Krutika Parab
Manan Badani
Pankaj Kadam

Copy Editors
Sayanee Mukherjee
Laxmi Subramanian

Project Coordinator
Sageer Parkar

Proofreader
Linda Morris

Indexers
Mehreen Deshmukh
Tejal R. Soni

Graphics
Ronak Dhruv

Production Coordinator
Conidon Miranda

Cover Work
Conidon Miranda

About the Author

Ray Rischpater is an engineer and author with over 20 years' experience writing about and developing for computing platforms.

During this time, he has participated in the development of Internet technologies and custom applications for Java ME, Qualcomm BREW, Apple iPhone, Google Android, Palm OS, Newton, and Magic Cap, as well as several proprietary platforms. Presently, he's employed as a senior engineer at Microsoft in Mountain View, working on mapping and data visualization.

When not writing for or about mobile platforms, he enjoys hiking and photography with his family and friends in and around the San Lorenzo Valley in central California. When he's able, he also provides a public service through amateur radio as the licensed Amateur Extra station KF6GPE.

The books he's written so far include:

- *Microsoft Mapping: Geospatial Development with Bing Maps and C#* (with *Carmen Au*, *Apress, 2013*)
- *Beginning Nokia Apps Development* (with *Daniel Zucker*, *Apress, 2010*)
- *Beginning Java ME Platform* (*Apress, 2008*)
- *Wireless Web Development, Second Edition* (*Apress, 2004*)
- *eBay Application Development* (*Apress, 2004*)
- *Software Development for the QUALCOMM BREW Platform* (*Apress, 2003*)
- *Wireless Web Development, First Edition* (*Apress, 2002*)
- *Internet Appliances: A Wiley Tech Brief* (*John Wiley & Sons, 2001*)
- *Advanced Palm Programming* (with *Steve Mann*, *John Wiley & Sons, 2000*)
- *Palm Enterprise Applications: A Wiley Tech Brief* (*John Wiley & Sons, 2000*)

He holds a bachelor's degree in pure mathematics from the University of California, Santa Cruz and is a member of the IEEE, ACM, and ARRL.

www.PacktPub.com

Support files, eBooks, discount offers and more

You might want to visit `www.PacktPub.com` for support files and downloads related to your book.

Did you know that Packt offers eBook versions of every book published, with PDF and ePub files available? You can upgrade to the eBook version at `www.PacktPub.com` and as a print book customer, you are entitled to a discount on the eBook copy. Get in touch with us at `service@packtpub.com` for more details.

At `www.PacktPub.com`, you can also read a collection of free technical articles, sign up for a range of free newsletters and receive exclusive discounts and offers on Packt books and eBooks.

`http://PacktLib.PacktPub.com`

Do you need instant solutions to your IT questions? PacktLib is Packt's online digital book library. Here, you can access, read and search across Packt's entire library of books.

Why Subscribe?

- Fully searchable across every book published by Packt
- Copy and paste, print and bookmark content
- On demand and accessible via web browser

Free Access for Packt account holders

If you have an account with Packt at `www.PacktPub.com`, you can use this to access PacktLib today and view nine entirely free books. Simply use your login credentials for immediate access.

Table of Contents

Preface	**1**
Chapter 1: Getting Started with Qt Creator	**7**
Downloading Qt Creator	7
Finding your way around Qt Creator	9
Your first application – Hello World	10
Hello World using the Qt GUI library	12
Hello World using Qt Quick	16
Summary	19
Chapter 2: Building Applications with Qt Creator	**21**
Getting started – our sample library	21
Learning the landscape – the Build menu and .pro files	24
Linking against our sample library	27
Getting lost and found again – debugging	31
Setting breakpoints and stepping through your program	33
Fine-grained control of breakpoints	36
Examining variables and memory	37
Examining the call stack	39
The Projects pane and building your project	41
A review – running and debugging your application	42
Summary	43
Chapter 3: Designing Your Application with Qt Designer	**45**
Code interlude – signals and slots	46
Creating forms in Qt Designer	49
Creating the main form	50
Using application resources	54
Instantiating forms, message boxes, and dialogs in your application	55

Wiring the Qt GUI application logic	**59**
Learning more about Qt GUI widgets	63
Code interlude – Qt Quick and QML syntax	**63**
Creating Qt Quick applications in Qt Designer	**66**
Creating a reusable button	67
The calculator's main view	70
Learning more about Qt Quick and QML	73
Summary	**74**
Chapter 4: Localizing Your Application with Qt Linguist	**75**
Understanding the task of localization	**75**
Marking strings for localization	**76**
Localizing your application with Qt Linguist	**77**
Including localized strings in your application	**80**
Localizing special things – currencies and dates with QLocale	**81**
Summary	**82**
Chapter 5: Performance Optimization with Qt Creator	**83**
The QML performance analyzer	**83**
QtSlowButton – a Qt Quick application in need of performance tuning	84
Finding memory leaks with Valgrind	**88**
QtLeakyButton – a Qt C++ application in need of memory help	89
Summary	**92**
Chapter 6: Developing Mobile Applications with Qt Creator	**93**
A mobile software development primer	**93**
User attention is at a premium	94
Computational resources are at a premium	95
Network resources are at a premium	96
Storage resources are at a premium	96
To port or not to port?	97
A word on testing	98
Setting up Qt Creator for Android	**98**
Downloading all the pieces	99
Setting up the environment variables	99
Finishing the Android SDK installation	100
Configuring Qt Creator	102
Building and running your application	103
Summary	**104**

Chapter 7: Qt Tips and Tricks — 105
- Writing console applications with Qt Creator — 105
- Integration with version control systems — 107
- Configuring coding style and coding format options — 109
- Building from the command line — 111
- Setting Qt Quick window display options — 112
- Learning more about Qt — 114
- Summary — 116

Index — 117

Preface

Whether you're just getting started with programming, or you've settled on Qt as the GUI toolkit for your project, Qt Creator is a great choice for an Integrated Development Environment (IDE)! In this book, we work to help you make the most of Qt Creator, showing you almost every facet of using Qt Creator, from its configuration through compiling and debugging applications, along with numerous tips and tricks. Along the way, you gain valuable experience not just with Qt Creator as an IDE, but with Qt and Qt Quick as well. After reading this book, you'll be able to:

- Edit, compile, debug, and run C++ applications using Qt Creator, opening a path to build state-of-the-art console and GUI applications with Qt and the Standard Template Library (STL)
- Edit, compile, debug, and run Qt Quick applications using Qt Creator, giving you access to one of the most advanced declarative GUI authoring environments anywhere
- Design GUI applications using Qt Designer to build either traditional widget-based or Qt Quick applications
- Analyze the memory and runtime performance of your Qt applications, and make improvements, and fix defects
- Provide localized versions of your application, so that you can deploy it all over the world in different languages
- Use Qt Quick and Qt Widgets to write mobile applications for platforms such as Google Android

What this book covers

This book is divided into seven chapters, which you should plan on reading in order, especially if you're new to Qt Creator and Qt programming in general. These chapters are:

Chapter 1, Getting Started with Qt Creator, explains how to download and install Qt Creator, as well as edit simple applications to test your installation.

Chapter 2, Building Applications with Qt Creator, explains how to compile, run, and debug your application using Qt Creator. You will learn how Qt Creator integrates with both the GNU debugger and the Microsoft console debugger to provide breakpoints, memory inspection, and other debugging help.

Chapter 3, Designing Your Application with Qt Designer, explains how to use the drag-and-drop GUI designer that is part of Qt Creator, to build both Qt widget-based and Qt Quick applications.

Chapter 4, Localizing Your Application with Qt Linguist, explains how to manage resource strings for different locales, letting you build your application with different languages in different locales.

Chapter 5, Performance Optimization with Qt Creator, explains how to use Qt Creator to examine your Qt Quick application's runtime performance, as well as how to perform memory profiling of your application with Valgrind, an open source diagnostic tool.

Chapter 6, Developing Mobile Applications with Qt Creator, gives a look at the exciting arena of mobile software development, and shows how you can use what you've learned in this book about Qt and Qt Creator to write applications for platforms such as Google Android.

Chapter 7, Qt Tips and Tricks, covers tricks for using Qt and Qt Creator that will help you use the Qt framework and the Qt Creator IDE efficiently.

What you need for this book

Qt and Qt Creator are cross-platform tools. Whether you're using a Windows machine, a Macintosh using Mac OS X, or a workstation running Linux, you probably have what you need. You should have a reasonable amount of disk space (around 10 gigabytes is plenty) to install the whole Qt Creator IDE and Qt libraries, and as with any software development environment, the more RAM you have, the better (although I've run Qt Creator on netbooks running Ubuntu with a gigabyte of RAM and survived!).

You should have a basic understanding of computer programming, and should be prepared to write code in C++. Basic knowledge of JavaScript is helpful if you're interested in programming with Qt Quick, but you can pick that up along the way with little difficulty.

Who this book is for

I wrote this book for those who have little or no experience with Qt and Qt Creator, who may be using it for the first time as part of a college class, an open source project, or who just want to experiment with the platform and IDE.

I especially want to encourage you to read this book if you're a student using Qt Creator in your university class on C++ programming! You should focus on the first two chapters, and as much of the rest as you need for your course.

Conventions

In this book, you will find a number of styles of text that distinguish between different kinds of information. Here are some examples of these styles, and an explanation of their meaning.

Code words in text, database table names, folder names, filenames, file extensions, pathnames, dummy URLs, user input, and Twitter handles are shown as follows: "For the name, enter `HelloWorldConsole`, and choose a path that makes sense for you (or accept the default)."

A block of code is set as follows:

```
#include <QCoreApplication>
#include <iostream>
using namespace std;
int main(int argc, char *argv[])
{
  QCoreApplication a(argc, argv);
  cout << "Hello world!";
  return a.exec();
}
```

When we wish to draw your attention to a particular part of a code block, the relevant lines or items are set in bold:

```
import QtQuick 2.0
Rectangle {
  width: 360
  height: 360
  Text {
    text: qsTr("Hello World")
    anchors.centerIn: parent
  }
  MouseArea {
    anchors.fill: parent
    onClicked: {
      Qt.quit();
    }
  }
}
```

New terms and **important words** are shown in bold. Words that you see on the screen, in menus or dialog boxes for example, appear in the text like this: "Where it says **Type Here**, right-click and choose **Remove menu bar**."

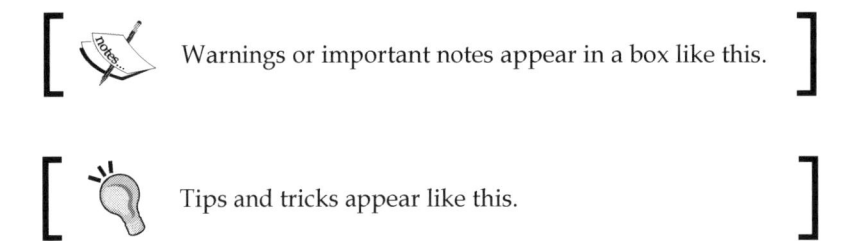

> Warnings or important notes appear in a box like this.

> Tips and tricks appear like this.

Reader feedback

Feedback from our readers is always welcome. Let us know what you think about this book—what you liked or may have disliked. Reader feedback is important for us to develop titles that you really get the most out of.

To send us general feedback, simply send an e-mail to feedback@packtpub.com, and mention the book title via the subject of your message.

If there is a topic that you have expertise in and you are interested in either writing or contributing to a book, see our author guide on www.packtpub.com/authors.

Customer support

Now that you are the proud owner of a Packt book, we have a number of things to help you to get the most from your purchase.

Downloading the example code

You can download the example code files for all Packt books you have purchased from your account at http://www.packtpub.com. If you purchased this book elsewhere, you can visit http://www.packtpub.com/support and register to have the files e-mailed directly to you.

Errata

Although we have taken every care to ensure the accuracy of our content, mistakes do happen. If you find a mistake in one of our books—maybe a mistake in the text or the code—we would be grateful if you would report this to us. By doing so, you can save other readers from frustration and help us improve subsequent versions of this book. If you find any errata, please report them by visiting http://www.packtpub.com/submit-errata, selecting your book, clicking on the **errata submission form** link, and entering the details of your errata. Once your errata are verified, your submission will be accepted and the errata will be uploaded on our website, or added to any list of existing errata, under the Errata section of that title. Any existing errata can be viewed by selecting your title from http://www.packtpub.com/support.

Piracy

Piracy of copyright material on the Internet is an ongoing problem across all media. At Packt, we take the protection of our copyright and licenses very seriously. If you come across any illegal copies of our works, in any form, on the Internet, please provide us with the location address or website name immediately so that we can pursue a remedy.

Please contact us at copyright@packtpub.com with a link to the suspected pirated material.

We appreciate your help in protecting our authors, and our ability to bring you valuable content.

Questions

You can contact us at questions@packtpub.com if you are having a problem with any aspect of the book, and we will do our best to address it.

1
Getting Started with Qt Creator

Qt Creator is the integrated software development environment that supports both traditional C++ application development, as well as development using the Qt project's libraries (collectively called "Qt", pronounced "cute"). In this chapter, we will see everything we need to get started with Qt Creator:

- Where to download Qt Creator for Linux, Mac OS X, or Windows
- How to ensure that your basic configuration is running
- A quick look at a simple Qt GUI application, as well as a Qt Quick application

Downloading Qt Creator

Qt, the cross-platform toolkit behind Qt Creator, has had a long and illustrious history. Presently, a project of Digia, it has its own URL at `qt-project.org` and has both commercial and noncommercial licenses available.

Getting Started with Qt Creator

To get started with the noncommercial version for free, head over to `http://bit.ly/13G4Jfr` to see something similar to the following screenshot:

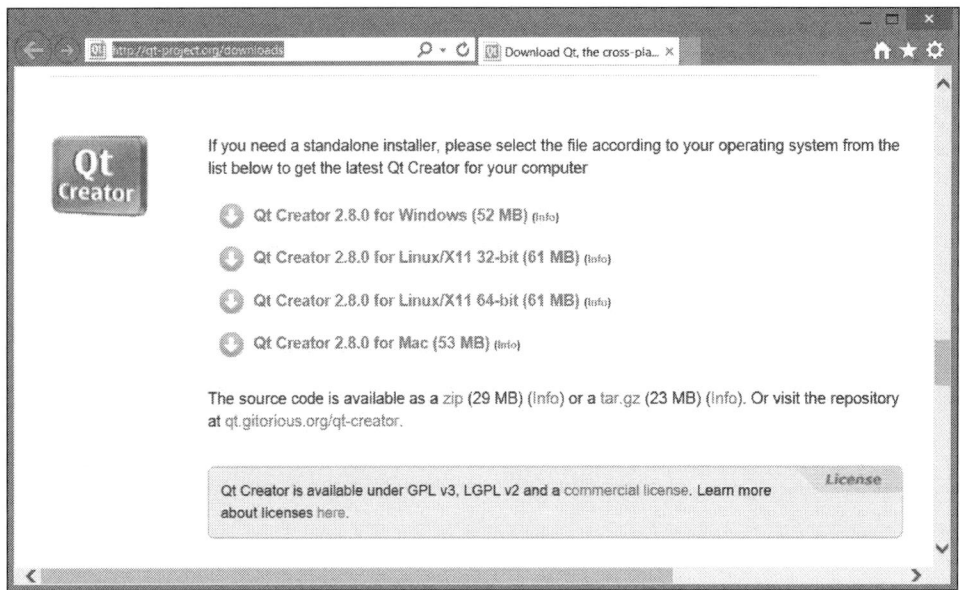

Downloading Qt Creator

One of the most popular platforms for application development with Qt is Linux. On many Linux variants—notably Ubuntu, my personal favorite—you can get Qt Creator using the package manager. On my Ubuntu box, Qt Creator is just a `sudo apt-get install qtcreator` command away. You'll get a version of Qt matched with your flavor of Linux, although it might not be the latest and greatest build from Digia.

We can also download bits and pieces of Qt, such as just the runtime libraries, or build Qt Creator from source. This typically requires that you already have a compiler and basic development tools installed, and a basic understanding of `qmake` and Qt's build configuration management system.

Some downloads include the C++ compiler and linker you need for your development; others don't. For example, on Windows there's a variant that includes the MinGW tool chain, so you have everything you need to build applications. However, you can also download Qt Creator for Windows that uses the Microsoft Visual Studio compilers, so, if you prefer using Visual Studio for your compilation and Qt Creator as your IDE, that's also an option. On Mac OS X, you'll need to have Xcode and the command-line development tools installed first; you can download Xcode from the Mac OS X App Store, and then use Xcode to download the command-line development tools.

Once the installer is downloaded, run it in the usual way. It'll launch an installation wizard for your platform, and typically the installation takes about three or four minutes. You'll want to have plenty of disk space. Qt Creator doesn't consume that much disk space, but software development typically does; figure at least 500 megabytes for the tools and libraries, and budget a few gigabytes free on your main drive for your source code, intermediate object files, debug symbols, and of course, your compiled application. (This is especially important to plan for if you're running Qt Creator on a virtual machine; make sure that the virtual hard drive for your virtual machine image has plenty of disk space.) You should also ensure that your development box has plenty of RAM; the more, the better. Qt Creator runs happily in 2 GB of RAM, but the compiler and linker used by Qt Creator can run a lot faster if it has more RAM available.

Finding your way around Qt Creator

The following screenshot shows what you see the first time you launch Qt Creator. Let's take a closer look at each portion of the screen:

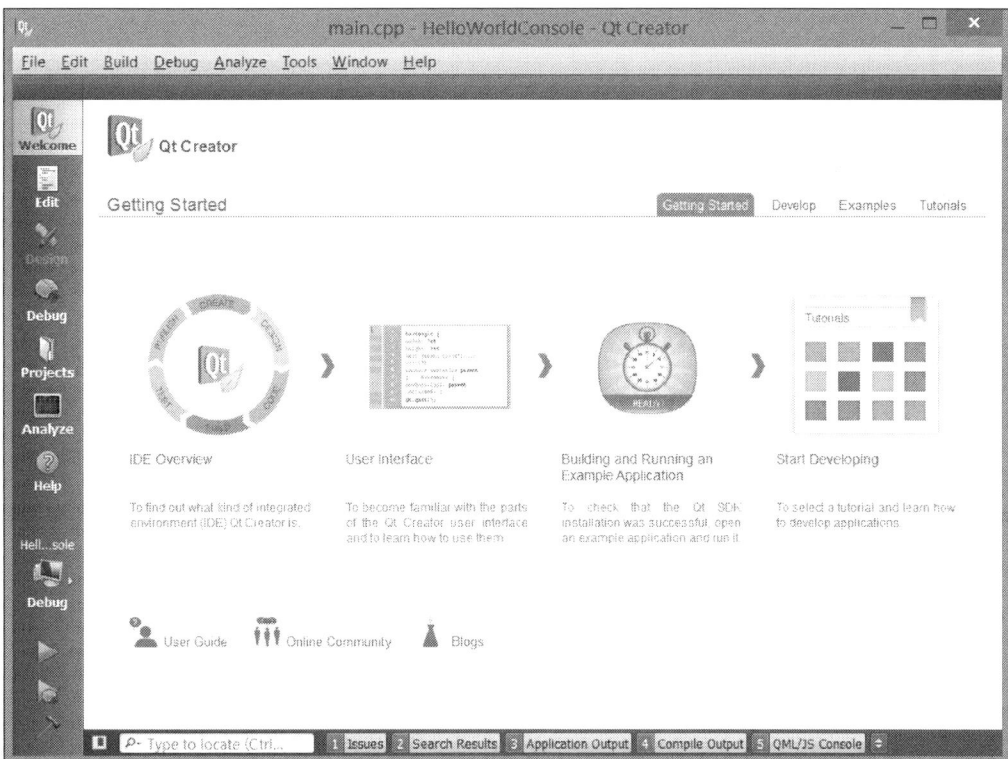

The landing page of Qt Creator

The main window, which currently shows the icons for **IDE Overview**, **User Interface**, **Building and Running an Example Application**, and **Start Developing**, is your workspace. Under normal conditions, this will be where you'll see the source code for your application. Along the left-hand side are a series of icons that let you select various views into your application. They are:

- The **Welcome** view shows basic information about Qt Creator
- The **Edit** view lets you edit the files that make up your application
- The **Design** view lets you use the Qt Designer to design the user interface for your application
- The **Debug** view lets you debug your application while it's running, including doing things like viewing memory and variables, setting breakpoints, and stepping through your application
- The **Projects** view lets you adjust the build and link settings for your project
- The **Analyze** view lets you profile your application's runtime performance
- The **Help** view provides documentation about Qt Creator and the Qt Framework

Below the **Help** view button in the previous screenshot you can see the active project; when I took this screenshot, I had already created our first application. Let's do that now.

Your first application – Hello World

In Qt Creator, choose **New File or Project...** from the **File** menu. Qt Creator will present you with the **New** project wizard, which lets you choose the kind of project you want to create, give it a name and so forth. To create our first application:

1. Choose **New File or Project...** if you haven't already.
2. Qt Creator presents you with a dialog that has a dizzying array of project choices. Choose **Application**, then **Qt Console Application**, and click on **Choose...**.
3. Qt Creator asks you for a name and a path to the directory where you want to store the files for the project. For the name, enter `HelloWorldConsole`, and choose a path that makes sense for you (or accept the default). Then, click on **Next**.
4. Qt Creator can support various kits and libraries against which to build an application. Select the desktop Qt kit that should have been installed by default, leaving both the **Release** and **Debug** choices checked. Then, click on **Next**.

5. In the next step, Qt Creator prompts you about version control for your project. Qt Creator can use your installed version control clients to perform change tracking for your project. For now, skip this and leave **Add to version control** set to **None** and click on **Finish**.

Qt Creator creates your project and switches to the **Edit** view. In the source code editor for the file main.cpp, enter the following code:

```cpp
#include <QCoreApplication>
#include <iostream>

using namespace std;

int main(int argc, char *argv[])
{
    QCoreApplication a(argc, argv);

    cout << "Hello world!";

    return a.exec();
}
```

The QCoreApplication task handles the system startup for an application, and every Qt Console app needs to create one and call its exec method, as part of the main method. It sets up Qt's event handler and provides a bunch of porting helpers to determine things such as your application directory, library paths, and other details.

For a console application, that's all you need: you can freely mix and match Qt classes with the C++ standard library and **Standard Template Library** (although once you master Qt's foundation classes, many STL constructs feel somewhat limiting).

Next, let's compile and run the application. There are several ways you can do this. You can use any one of the following options:

- Hit *F5* to build and run your application in the debugger
- Choose **Start Debugging...** from the **Debug** menu
- Click on the green **Run** arrow below the **Help** view button on the left to run the application
- Click on the green **Run** arrow with the bug over the arrow to debug the application

> If all you want to do is build the application, you can click on the hammer icon below the **Run** and **Debug** icons.

When you choose one of these options, Qt Creator invokes the compiler and linker to build your application. If you chose a debug option, Qt Creator switches to the **Debug** view (which I will discuss in detail in the next chapter) as it starts your application.

Once the application starts, you'll see the `Hello world!` message in the console view.

> **Downloading the example code**
> You can download the example code files for all Packt books you have purchased from your account at http://www.packtpub.com. If you purchased this book elsewhere, you can visit http://www.packtpub.com/support and register to have the files e-mailed directly to you.

Hello World using the Qt GUI library

One of Qt's strengths is its rich collection of GUI elements you can use to create windowed applications. Making a GUI application is similar, in principle, to making a console application; instead of choosing **Qt Console Application**, choose **Qt Gui Application** from the **New** dialog presented when you choose **New File or Project…**. Try that now:

1. First, close the current file and project by choosing **Close All Projects and Editors** from the **File** menu.
2. Next, choose **New File or Project…** again, and choose **Qt Gui Application** from the first step of the wizard.
3. Walk through the wizard again, naming your project `HelloWorldGui`.
4. The **New** project wizard will prompt you for the name of the class implementing your main window. Stick with the defaults given to you: leave the subclass as `QMainWindow`, and the name as `MainWindow`.

Qt Creator creates a default subclass of the class providing the platform's basic window handling in the `mainform.h` and `mainform.cpp` files, and creates a form that will contain the widgets for your application's window. If you run the application at this point, you'll see an empty window. Instead, double-click on the **Forms** folder in the second pane of Qt Creator, and then double-click on the file `mainwindow.ui`. Qt Creator switches to the **Design** view, and you'll see something similar to the following screenshot:

Chapter 1

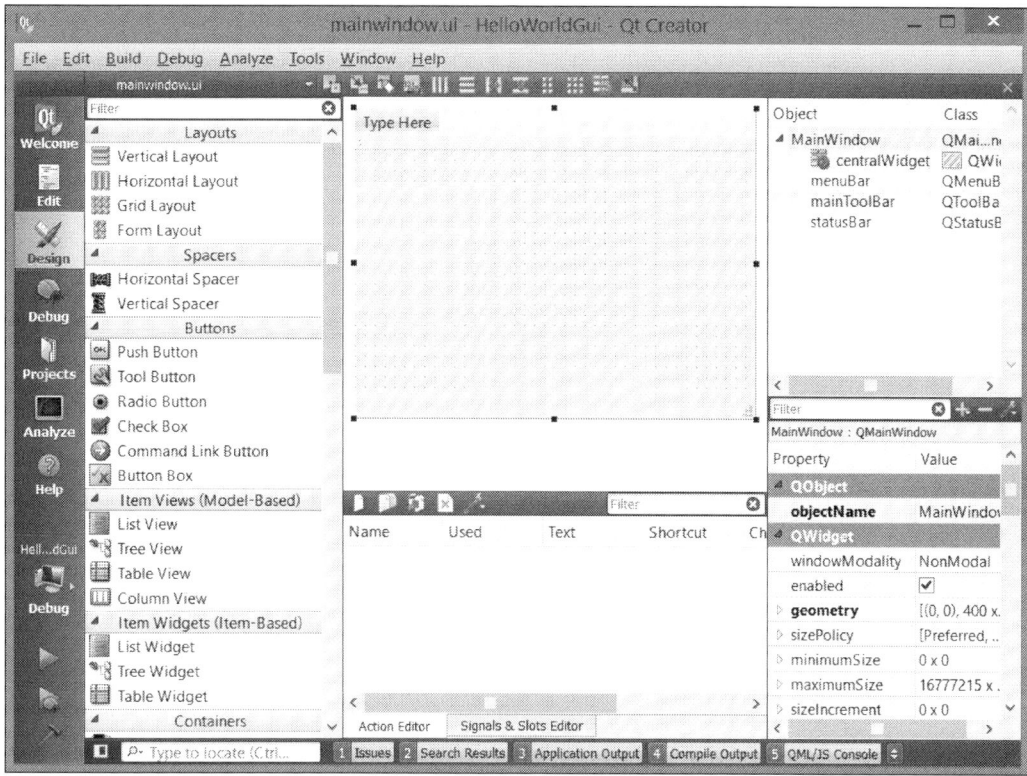

Qt Creator's Design view

To the left, is a list of layouts you can choose to organize widgets such as spacers, views, containers, buttons, and other widgets. In the middle, is a view of the layout of your application's main window, and to the right are panes with a hierarchy of the objects in your main window and the properties of any item you click in the main window.

While I explore Qt Designer more in *Chapter 3, Designing Your Application with Qt Designer*, you can get a feel for using it to build a simple UI:

1. Where it says **Type Here**, right-click and choose **Remove menu bar**.
2. Drag a label (under **Display Widgets** in the left-hand pane) and drop it on the window preview in the center pane.
3. Double-click on the label that appears and type, Hello world!.
4. Grab a corner of the label and resize it, so the entire text is shown. You can also move it around in the window.

Getting Started with Qt Creator

5. Note that when you click on the label, the properties field in the lower right corner updates to show the properties of your new label.
6. Drag a button (under **Buttons** in the left-hand pane) and drop it on the window preview in the center pane.
7. Double-click on the button and change its text to Exit.
8. With the new button selected, change the **objectName** field in the property browser to exitButton.
9. Right-click on the button and choose **Go to slot…**. A window appears with a list of slots (for now, you can think of a slot as something that is triggered on an action).
10. Choose **clicked()** from the list that appears.
11. Qt Creator returns to the **Edit** view for your mainindow.cpp file. Change it to read:

```
#include "mainwindow.h"
#include "ui_mainwindow.h"
#include <QApplication>
MainWindow::MainWindow(QWidget *parent) :
    QMainWindow(parent),
    ui(new Ui::MainWindow)
{
    ui->setupUi(this);
}

MainWindow::~MainWindow()
{
    delete ui;
}

void MainWindow::on_pushButton_clicked()
{
    QApplication::exit();
}
```

Before running your application, let's be sure we understand the implementation of the MainWindow class. The MainWindow class's constructor loads the description of the user interface for the main window and sets it up using the Qt Creator-generated class Ui::MainWindow. The destructor deletes the implementation of the code layout, and the on_pushButton_clicked method simply terminates the application by calling the static method exit implemented by the QApplication class.

Finally, we have to add the `on_pushButton_clicked` method declaration to `MainWindow.h`. Double-click on that file in the browser on the left and make sure it reads:

```
#ifndef MAINWINDOW_H
#define MAINWINDOW_H

#include <QMainWindow>

namespace Ui {
class MainWindow;
}

class MainWindow : public QMainWindow
{
    Q_OBJECT

public:
    explicit MainWindow(QWidget *parent = 0);
    ~MainWindow();

private slots:
    void on_pushButton_clicked();

private:
    Ui::MainWindow *ui;
};

#endif // MAINWINDOW_H
```

The key lines you need to add are:

```
private slots:
    void on_pushButton_clicked();
```

We'll learn more about signals and slots in the next chapter; for now, it's enough to know that you're declaring a private function to be triggered when you click on the button.

Run the application. It should open a single window with the text **Hello World**; clicking on the **Exit** button in the window (or the close box on the upper-right corner) should close the application. At this point, if you think you want to learn more about Qt GUI widget applications, go ahead and try dragging other GUI items to the window, or explore the help for Qt GUI applications by switching to the **Help** view and choosing **Qt Gui** from the list of help items.

Hello World using Qt Quick

Qt Quick is Qt's newer declarative framework for the user interface, and with it it's incredibly easy to create fluid applications with animated transitions and flowing user interfaces. Using Qt Quick, you describe your user interface using QML, a JavaScript-like language that lets you declare the user interface elements and how they relate; the Qt Quick runtime does most of the heavy lifting in the implementation of your application.

By now, you can guess how to create a Qt Quick project: choose **New File or Project...** from the **File** menu, and then click on **Qt Quick 2 Application (Built-in Types)** and follow the wizard.

The wizard will ask no additional questions, and if you just walk through the wizard, you end up with a simple application that actually displays `Hello World` in its own window. Here's the code it supplies:

```
import QtQuick 2.0

Rectangle {
    width: 360
    height: 360
    Text {
        text: qsTr("Hello World")
        anchors.centerIn: parent
    }
    MouseArea {
        anchors.fill: parent
        onClicked: {
            Qt.quit();
        }
    }
}
```

If you know JavaScript, the syntax of this may look a little familiar, but it's still different. The first line is an import statement; it indicates to the QML runtime what classes should be available. At a minimum, all of your Qt Quick applications must import QtQuick Version 2.0, as this one does.

The QML itself follows. It declares a parent rectangle of 360 × 360 pixels—that determines the size of the application window. Inside the rectangle are two objects: **Text** and **MouseArea**. The **Text** object is just a label with the text `Hello World`, placed in the center of the rectangle. Note that the value of the text property is actually the result of a function call, a call to the function `qsTr`, Qt's built-in localization function, which looks at application resources to return the localized version of `Hello World` if it's been provided.

Chapter 1

The **MouseArea** object takes user input and can execute functions based on that input; it's sized to fit the parent (`anchors.fill` is set to `parent`) and responds when clicked by executing the function assigned to the `onClicked` property. This `onClicked` function just exits the application by calling the Qt class's `quit` function.

At this point, you can run the application in the usual way, and you'll see a window with the text **Hello World** centered in it.

While the principles are similar, the Qt Quick Designer is very different from the Qt GUI Designer; have a look at the following screenshot:

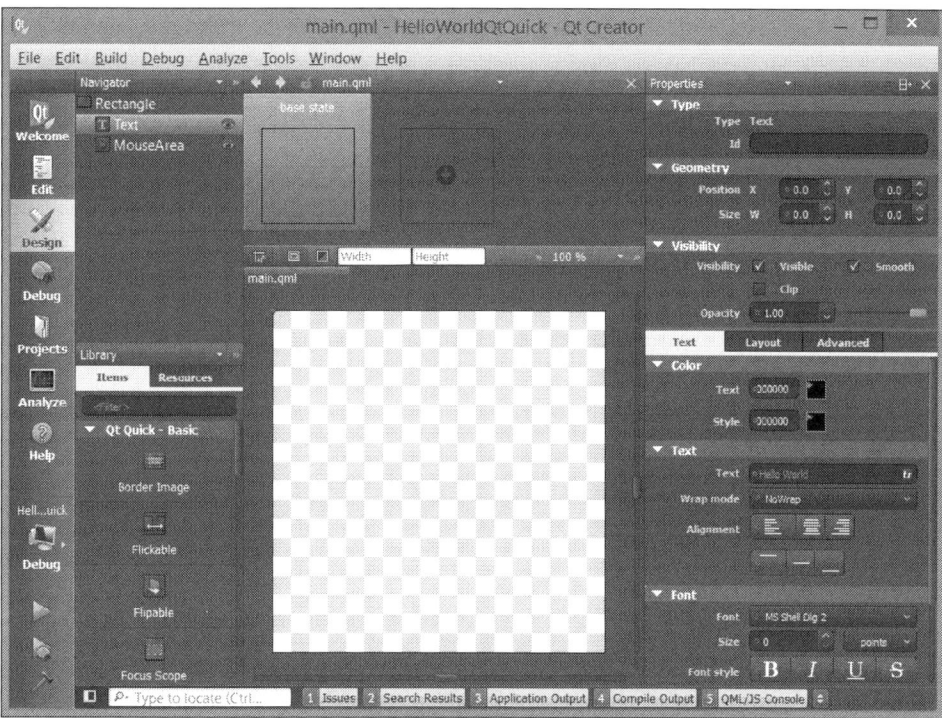

The Qt Quick Designer

There are some obvious similarities. Both designers show a list of things you can add to a view, along with a hierarchy of objects in the view and the properties of individual objects. However, there are far fewer Qt Quick widgets than Qt GUI widgets, and the widgets in Qt Quick don't match the look and feel of the native platform to nearly the same extent. By design, Qt GUI is meant for building conventional applications that match the native platform, while Qt Quick is used for creating device-independent applications with their own look and feel. For example, you'd probably write an enterprise data collection application using Qt GUI, while you'd create a media center application using Qt Quick.

[17]

Using the designer is the same in both cases, however. Let's add another **MouseArea** to the main view, and give it something to do:

1. Select `main.qml` in the list of files in Qt Creator and click on **Design** to see the **Design** view.
2. On the **Library** pane, select items and scroll down until you see **Rectangle**. Drag the rectangle to the center pane and drop it somewhere above the `Hello World` label. You may need to resize the rectangle so that the label is still visible.
3. With the rectangle selected in the window pane, under **Colors**, enter a color for your rectangle.
4. Now drag a **MouseArea** object out of the **Library** pane, and drop it on your new rectangle.
5. With the **MouseArea** selected, choose **Layout** and mouse over the layouts until you see **Fill to Parent**. Click on it.
6. Go back to the **Edit** view and modify `main.qml` to look like the following:

   ```
   import QtQuick 2.0

   Rectangle {
       width: 360
       height: 360
       Text {
           id: text
           text: qsTr("Hello World")
           anchors.centerIn: parent
       }
       MouseArea {
           anchors.fill: parent
           onClicked: {
               Qt.quit();
           }

           Rectangle {
               id: rectangle1
               x: 80
               y: 7
               width: 200
               height: 124
               color: "#777777"
   ```

```
            MouseArea {
                id: mousearea1
                anchors.fill: parent
                onClicked: text.text = qsTr("Hi there!")
            }
        }
    }
}
```

You should see that most of the changes were made by the **Design** view; it added a rectangle inside the original **MouseArea** object, and another **MouseArea** inside that. You should need to add the line giving the text element an ID of text, and the onClicked handler to the new **MouseArea** object that you dragged out in the **Design** view. The id property lets other QML access the text field by name (in this case, its name is simply text), and the onClicked handler changes the contents of the text item's text property to the text Hi there!.

It's worth making an observation about qsTr here: you don't have to add any text to the application resources to get basic localization working. This is unlike most other platforms, where localization occurs by providing keys to values in local files for strings with a default value for the unlocalized strings.

Run the application. You'll see your rectangle above the text **Hello World**, and clicking on the rectangle changes the text to read **Hi there!**.

Summary

Getting Qt Creator is easy; it's just a web download away, or on most Linux platforms, it's an optional installation through the native package manager (although the versions delivered by a package manager may be slightly older than what you get from the Qt Project's website).

Qt Creator organizes its source code for you in projects; when you first launch it you can either create a default project, or create a new project to contain the source code and resources for your application. Inside Qt Creator are all the options you need to compile and debug your application. In addition, it supports designer tools for developing both Qt GUI and Qt Quick applications.

In the next, chapter we'll dig into the details of how to configure Qt Creator for compiling and editing your code, including how to add source files to your project, configure compiler and linker options, add dependencies to third-party libraries, and so on.

2
Building Applications with Qt Creator

The first thing you're going to want to do with Qt Creator is figure out how to add source files and build (or debug) your project. This chapter is all about that—we'll go over how to add files to your project, how to create libraries to your project, and use the debugger and console logger. At the end of this chapter, you'll be driving Qt Creator to develop your console applications like a pro.

Getting started – our sample library

This chapter's example code has two pieces: a library that defines a public function and a console application that calls that function. Libraries are a great way to break up your applications, and while this example is trivial, it also lets me show you how to create a library and include it in your application.

I'm going to stretch your imagination a bit: let's pretend that you're responsible for setting up a library of math functions. In this example, we'll only write one function, `factorial`. You should remember the `factorial` function from introductory programming; it's represented by *a!*, and is defined as:

- 0! is 0
- 1! is 1
- *n!* is $n \times (n-1)!$

This is a recursive definition, and we can code it this way:

```
unsigned long factorial(unsigned int n)
{
    switch(n)
    {
        case 0: return 0;
        case 1: return 1;
        default: return n * factorial(n-1);
    }
}
```

> An alternate definition that avoids the cost of function calls is:
> ```
> unsigned long factorial(unsigned int n)
> {
>     unsigned long result = 1;
>     for(unsigned int i = n; i > 1; i--)
>     {
>         result *= i;
>     }
> }
> ```

Why did I pick the recursive definition? Three reasons: I think that it's clearer, function-call performance overhead isn't a big deal in this example, and many readers of this book may be using this book as part of introductory computer science courses where recursion is taught and should be reinforced.

Let's begin by creating the library that implements our `factorial` function. To do this:

1. In Qt Creator, from the **File** menu, choose **New File or Project…**.
2. Choose **Libraries** in the left-hand pane of the dialog and **C++ Library** from the center pane.
3. Qt Creator can create dynamic libraries (DLLs, in Windows parlance), static libraries, or plugins that can be shared between applications. We're going to create a static library, so in the next screen choose **Statically Linked Library**, and name it `MathFunctions`. Choose a reasonable path for the project.
4. In the next step of the wizard, leave the Qt version, **Debug**, and **Release** items checked.
5. Libraries built by Qt Creator can rely on the Qt libraries themselves. Let's allow this library to rely on QtCore, the core data structures for Qt; in the **Select Required Modules** window, leave **QtCore** checked and click on **Next**.

6. In the next window, you'll name the skeleton files that Qt Creator will add to your project. Click on **Next**.

7. In the **Project Management** window, choose **<None>** for the version control choice (we won't use version control for this project) and click on **Finish**.

8. Edit `mathfunctions.h` to include a static method declaration for our `factorial` function:

```
#ifndef MATHFUNCTIONS_H
#define MATHFUNCTIONS_H

class MathFunctions
{
public:
    MathFunctions();

    static unsigned long int factorial(unsigned int n);
};

#endif // MATHFUNCTIONS_H
```

9. Open `mathfunctions.cpp`. You can do this one of two ways, by either double-clicking on it in the **Projects** pane, or by right-clicking on the `factorial` function and choosing **Switch Header/Source**. Write your `factorial` function; `mathfunctions.cpp` should read:

```
#include "mathfunctions.h"

MathFunctions::MathFunctions()
{
}

unsigned long
MathFunctions::factorial(unsigned int n)
{
    switch(n)
    {
        case 0: return 0;
        case 1: return 1;
        default: return n * factorial(n-1);
    }
}
```

10. Click on the **Projects** button on the left, and change the output path for the **Release** and **Debug** builds to point to the same directory, by editing the **Build directory** line under **General**, first for the **Release** and then for **Debug** build configurations. To do this, remove the `release` and `debug` portions of the directory path from the **Build directory** path. This way, when you build your library, Qt Creator will place release and debug builds of your library in a single folder instead of folders named `release` and `debug`, respectively.

As you write the code, note that Qt Creator prompts you at various stages about things it can deduce from your header with automatic suggestions (called **autosuggest**). For example, once you type `MathFunc`, it offers to autocomplete the class name or the C pre-processor guard; you can select either using the mouse, or just hit *Enter* to get the class name. Similarly, typing the double colons tells Qt Creator you're trying to enter something in the `MathFunctions` class, and prompts you with the `MathFunctions` class members; you can use the arrows to select `factorial` and hit *Enter*, and it types that. Finally, typing an opening parenthesis cues Qt Creator that you're defining a function, and prompts you with the arguments to that function you defined in the header file. You'll see this autocompletion a lot when you type code; it's a great way to learn Qt, too, because you can type a class name or part of a function name and Qt Creator prompts you with helpful hints along the way.

Before you continue, be sure you've built your library in both the release and debug configurations. The easiest way to do this is to click on the build selector on the bottom left and choose either **Release** or **Debug**, and then click on the hammer icon to perform a build.

Learning the landscape – the Build menu and .pro files

In the previous chapter, you learned how to build applications by hitting the hammer button in the corner of Qt Creator's main window, or by starting the debugger. To just build your library—or any application—you can either use the hammer icon or various choices in the **Build** menu. The obvious choice is either **Build All** or **Rebuild All**; choosing **Build All** recompiles only those files that Qt Creator recognizes as those that need to be rebuilt; **Rebuild All** cleans the project of all object files and rebuilds the entire project from scratch. In most cases, it's sufficient to choose **Build All**, and that's what you want to do, because it's faster. Sometimes you really do want to rebuild the whole project, when Qt's `make` system can't reconcile all the dependencies (or, you've made changes to the dependencies). Choose **Build All** now, and wait for it to build while we discuss the other options.

The **Build** menu lets you build a single file—handy, if all you want to do is check the syntax of the code you're writing and make sure you're free of errors—or the entire project. It also lets you run the project outside of the debugger, which you might want to do in some circumstances, like giving a demonstration. You can also clean your project (remove all object files and other autogenerated products) by choosing **Clean All**. The **Publish** option is available for some add-on kits that let you publish compiled applications and libraries to application stores and repositories; you can find more details about that in the documentation of any Qt Creator add-in, such as the SDKs for Maemo development (an older Linux variant from Nokia for handheld devices).

Behind every Qt Creator project is a `.pro` file; this serves the same function as a `make` file, and, in fact, is processed by a Qt toolkit command called `qmake`. (Make files are files processed by the `make` command, which indicate what files should be compiled in what order to generate an executable.) These files are declarative, in that you declare the relationship between the files that make up your application, and `qmake` figures out how to build your application from there. In most cases you'll need to make few or no changes to a `.pro` file, but it doesn't hurt to understand how they work. Double-click on `MathFunctions.pro`, and you'll find:

```
#-------------------------------------------------
#
# Project created by QtCreator 2013-07-23T19:50:46
#
#-------------------------------------------------

QT       -= gui

TARGET = MathFunctions
TEMPLATE = lib
CONFIG += staticlib


SOURCES += mathfunctions.cpp

HEADERS += mathfunctions.h
unix:!symbian {
    maemo5 {
        target.path = /opt/usr/lib
    } else {
        target.path = /usr/lib
    }
    INSTALLS += target
}
```

The basic syntax of a `.pro` file is variable assignments; this file, generated by Qt Creator for us, assigns the following variables:

- The `QT` variable indicates the Qt modules your project will link against. By default, all projects include QtCore and QtGui; there's a plethora of other modules available, which include key features such as the WebKit web browsing engine (`QtWebkit`) and multimedia libraries (`Phonon`). Our assignment here, indicates that we use the default Qt modules, but don't link against `QtGui`.
- The `TARGET` variable is the name of the compiled library or executable.
- The `TEMPLATE` variable indicates the kind of `qmake` template `qmake` should use to generate the binary; in our case, we're saying it should use the template to create a `lib` file—a library.
- The `CONFIG` variable passes an additional configuration to the template of `qmake`; here, we say that we want a statically linked library.
- The `SOURCES` and `HEADERS` variables contain lists of the source and header files that make up your project.
- The `INSTALLS` variable indicates where the resulting build product should be installed. Here, it's set in a scope. Scopes let you specify conditional options in `qmake`; the condition for the scope is a variable or expression, which may be `true` or `false`, and the code that follows is executed if the variable is `true`. The scope at the end of this file says, "If we're building for a `unix` variant and the variant isn't `symbian`, set the `target.path` variable to `/opt/usr/lib` if the `unix` variant is `maemo`, otherwise set it to `/usr/lib` for other `unix` variants, and in either case, set the `INSTALLS` variable to `target`".

These are the basic variables you'll find in almost any `.pro` file; for a good discussion of `qmake` scopes you can use to control conditional compilation, see `http://bit.ly/163tAIh`. Two additional variables you're likely to want to know about are `DEFINES` and `LIBS`; `DEFINES` lets you specify preprocessor defines that should be set throughout the build process, and `LIBS` indicates additional libraries against which Qt Creator should link your project.

Note how variables are managed: you use `=` for assignment, `+=` to add an item to a list, and `-=` to remove an item from a list.

Linking against our sample library

Now, let's make an application that depends on our library. Our application will call the `factorial` function in the library, statically linking to the library to access the `factorial` function. To accomplish this, you need to:

1. Choose **Close All Projects and Editors** from the **File** menu.
2. Choose **New File or Project...** from the **File** menu, and create a new Qt console application called `MathFunctionsTest` using the wizard.
3. Right-click on **MathFunctionsTest**, and choose **Add Library**. You can then choose a library in your build tree, one outside your build tree, or an external library on your system like the Unix math library, `ffmpeg`, or another library you've created. Choose **External Library** and click on **Next**.
4. Browse to the library file that was built in the previous section by clicking on **Browse** next to the line labeled **Library file**. It'll be in a folder named something like `build-MathFunctions-Desktop_Qt_5_0_2_MSVC2012_64bit` in your project's folder. Choose the `MathFunctions` library in either the `release` or `debug` folders—it doesn't matter which.
5. Browse to include files for your library by clicking on **Browse** next to **Include path**; this is the directory where you put the headers for your library.
6. Choose static linking; if you were linking a dynamically linked library, of course you'd choose **Dynamic**.
7. Leave the other values set to their defaults, click on **Next** and then on **Finish**.

Qt Creator will work its magic with your .pro file, adding a `LIBS` variable that includes the output of your library build and an include path to your library's header files.

We can now call our `factorial` function. Edit `main.cpp` to read:

```
#include <QCoreApplication>
#include "MathFunctions.h"

int main(int argc, char *argv[])
{
    QCoreApplication a(argc, argv);

    qDebug("6! is %d", MathFunctions::factorial(6));

    return a.exec();
}
```

This code first includes our library header file. Note that if you compile the application after adding just the `#include` declaration, you'll get autosuggest help for every element of the `MathFunctions` library. This code uses `qDebug` instead of the C standard library to perform its console output.

> The `qDebug()` function actually has a stream-savvy implementation too. I could have written the `qDebug` line as
>
> ```
> qDebug() << "6! is" << MathFunctions::factorial(6);
> ```
>
> and the code would have generated the same output.

Now, build and run the application in debug mode; you should see a console window with the text `6! is 720`. Try building and running the library in release mode; wait, why is the debugging output from `qDebug` still there?

`qDebug` isn't really a debugging log, it's an output stream for debugging information regardless of build levels. If you want to turn off its output in release builds, you'll need to edit the `.pro` file. Double-click on your `.pro` file, and add the line:

```
CONFIG(release, debug|release): DEFINES += QT_NO_DEBUG_OUTPUT
```

This is another scope: it says that if your build configuration is release, add the preprocessor definition `QT_NO_DEBUG_OUTPUT` to the list of preprocessor definitions for the project.

Now, if you rebuild (don't just choose build, but actually choose rebuild, because you want a clean build through the entire system) and run in release mode, you won't see any output.

> Qt actually defines four output streams, one for debugging messages and one for bona fide warnings. Use `qDebug` for regular logging and `qWarning` to output messages of a higher priority. There's also `qCritical` and `qFatal` for higher-priority log messages that should indicate critical failures, or failures that cause the application to terminate. You can also turn off warnings in release builds the same way; simply add the following to your `.pro` file:
>
> ```
> CONFIG(release, debug|release): DEFINES += QT_NO_WARNING_OUTPUT
> ```

What if you want to add files to your project? You can either do it by manually editing the .pro file, which can be faster if you're a good typist, but also error prone and result in weird build problems if you mess up, or right-click on your project and choose either **Add New...** or **Add Existing Files...**. The **Add New...** option opens up a short wizard with choices like these:

- C++ header and source files
- Qt Designer forms that we'll talk about in the next chapter
- Qt Resource files that we'll talk about in the next chapter
- Qt Quick Markup (QML) files
- JavaScript files (which can contain the code implementing the logic of a Qt Quick application)
- OpenGL shaders for fragments or vertices in either full OpenGL or OpenGL/ES
- Text files (like a Readme file for your project) or a scratch file to use as a place to stash temporary clipboard items until you're done with an editing session

Before we move on to the important topic of debugging, let's look at one more .pro file, the .pro file for our application:

```
#-------------------------------------------------
#
# Project created by QtCreator 2013-07-23T20:43:19
#
#-------------------------------------------------

QT       += core

QT       -= gui


CONFIG(release, debug|release): DEFINES += QT_NO_DEBUG_OUTPUT

TARGET = MathFunctionsTest
CONFIG   += console
CONFIG   -= app_bundle

TEMPLATE = app

SOURCES += main.cpp
```

```
win32:CONFIG(release, debug|release): LIBS += -L$$PWD/../build-
MathFunctions-Desktop_Qt_5_0_2_MSVC2012_64bit/release/ -lMathFunctions
else:win32:CONFIG(debug, debug|release): LIBS += -L$$PWD/../build-
MathFunctions-Desktop_Qt_5_0_2_MSVC2012_64bit/debug/ -lMathFunctions
else:unix: LIBS += -L$$PWD/../build-MathFunctions-Desktop_Qt_5_0_2_
MSVC2012_64bit/ -lMathFunctions

INCLUDEPATH += $$PWD/../MathFunctions
DEPENDPATH += $$PWD/../MathFunctions

win32:CONFIG(release, debug|release): PRE_TARGETDEPS += $$PWD/../
build-MathFunctions-Desktop_Qt_5_0_2_MSVC2012_64bit/release/
MathFunctions.lib
else:win32:CONFIG(debug, debug|release): PRE_TARGETDEPS += $$PWD/../
build-MathFunctions-Desktop_Qt_5_0_2_MSVC2012_64bit/debug/
MathFunctions.lib
else:unix: PRE_TARGETDEPS += $$PWD/../build-MathFunctions-Desktop_
Qt_5_0_2_MSVC2012_64bit-Debug/libMathFunctions.a
```

Phew! That's pretty dense. Let's see if we can unravel it. It begins by telling the build system that we use QtCore, but not QtGui. Next up, is the instruction to disable the `qDebug` messages in release builds, which won't happen by default. The `TARGET`, `CONFIG`, and `TEMPLATE` options together say that we're building a console application with the name `MathFunctionsTest`. The next line indicates that we have one source file, `main.cpp`.

The next set of scopes indicates the path to our library, and handles the fact that our libraries are in different directories on Windows for `release` and `debug`—this is different from on Unix systems, where there is only one `build` variant of the library. After that, comes the `INCLUDEPATH` and `DEPENDPATH` variables, which indicate that there are library headers in the `MathFunctions` directory, and that the application depends on those headers. So, if the timestamps on the headers change, the binary should rebuild. The final scope specifies the same dependency on the output library itself; if the library changes, the application executable has to be rebuilt. This is especially important, because that way we can run multiple copies of Qt Creator, edit our library and application files separately, building the bits we need of either after they change. When we do so that way, all the dependencies get figured out and the right bits of the library and application get built automatically.

Getting lost and found again – debugging

Qt Creator has a state-of-the-art GUI that hooks into either the GNU debugger GDB, or Microsoft's command-line debugger CDB, if you use Microsoft tools.

If you've installed Qt Creator on Mac OS or Linux, or the MinGW version of Qt Creator for Windows, you have everything you need to begin debugging your application. If you already had Microsoft Visual Studio installed and installed a version of Qt Creator that uses Microsoft's compiler, you need to also install the Microsoft command-line debugger to use Qt Creator's debugging features. Here's how to install the command-line debugger:

1. Download the debugging tools for Windows, at either `http://bit.ly/1dWoqi0` if you are using the 32-bit version of the compiler and Qt Creator, or `http://bit.ly/12kEtGt` for the 64-bit version of the compiler and Qt Creator.
2. Configure the debugging symbol server by going to **Options** under the **Tools** menu, choosing the **Debugger** item on the left, choosing the **CDB** pane, and clicking on **Edit** next to the **Symbol Paths** line.

> Usually, the debugger works out of the box with Qt Creator, unless you're using the Microsoft toolchain. However, if you encounter problems, consult the Qt documentation on setting up the debugger at `http://bit.ly/19jgycQ`.

Building Applications with Qt Creator

The following screenshot shows the debugger in action with our test project, stopped at a breakpoint:

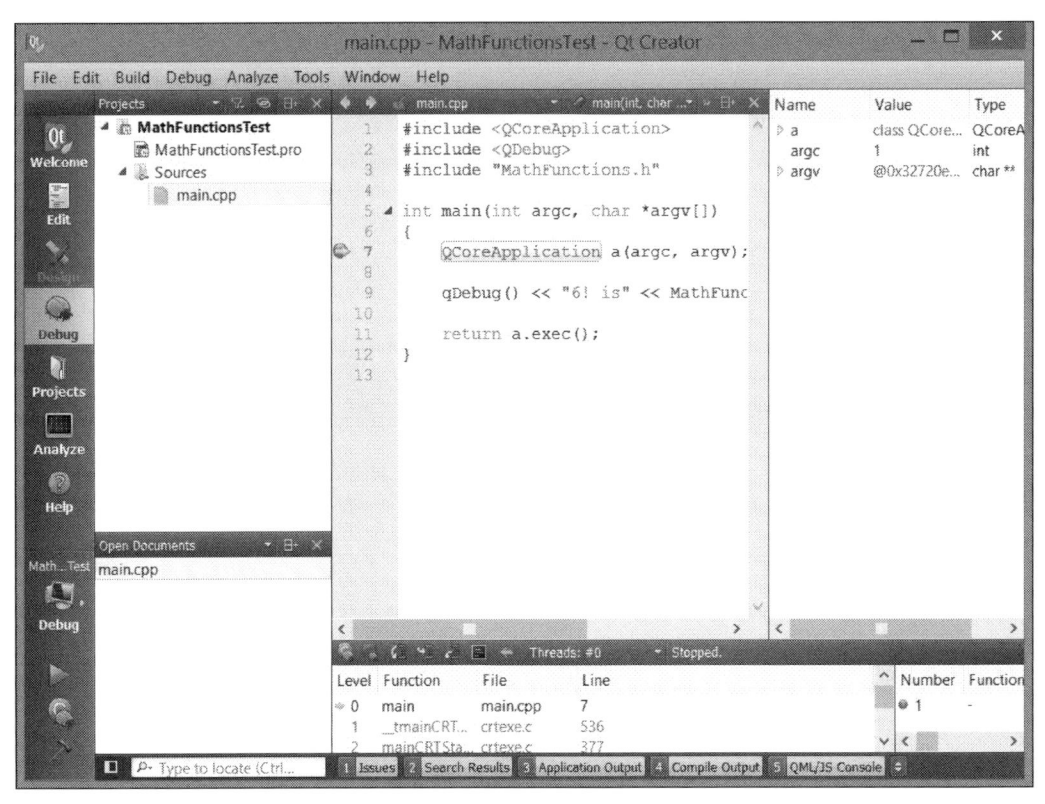

Qt Creator's Debug view in action

Let's look at the screenshot in detail to get oriented:

- On the left is the usual row of buttons to pick a view in Qt Creator
- Next to the buttons is the view of the project files and the list of open documents
- In the main editor pane, every source line has a clickable indicator to let you set and clear breakpoints
- The call stack, indicating how the program got to the line execution is stopped at, is shown in the pane below the editor pane

- On the upper right is the variable inspector, where you can see the values of the variables in the current stack frame, along with any global variables
- Below the variable inspector is a list of pending breakpoints, so you can turn on and off breakpoints without needing to hunt through the code

To generate the previous screenshot, I clicked on the left of line **7**, placing a breakpoint, and then clicked on the **Debug** button on the left after ensuring I'd specified a debug build in the build selector. Qt Creator built the application in debug mode, started the application, and let it run to the breakpoint on line **7**.

Setting breakpoints and stepping through your program

A breakpoint, if you haven't encountered the idea before, is just that—a point at which execution breaks and you can examine the program's state. Once stopped at a breakpoint, you can step into a function, or step over a line, executing your program one line at a time to see how it's behaving. In the **Debug** view, clicking on the left of the number line lets you set or clear breakpoints. While stopped at a breakpoint, a yellow arrow in the margin of the editor pane indicates the line of code that the processor is about to execute.

While at a breakpoint, several buttons appear above the call stack pane that let you control program flow. They are:

- The green continue button, which continues execution at the line indicated by the arrow. You can also continue by pressing the *F5* function key.
- The red stop button, which stops debugging altogether.
- The step over button, which executes the current line and advances to the next line before stopping again. You can step over one line by pressing *F10*.
- The step into button, which enters the next function to be called and stops again. You can step into a function by pressing *F11*.
- The step out button, which runs the remainder of the function in the current calling context before stopping again. You can step out of the current function by pressing *F11*.
- The instruction-wise button (which looks like a little screen), which toggles the debugger between working a source line at a time and an assembly line at a time.
- There's also a menu of threads, so you can see which thread is running or stopped.

If (in the previous screenshot) from line **7** we step over line **8** (pressing *F10*) and then press *F11*, we'll end up inside our `factorial` function, as you see in the next screenshot. I've clipped the screenshot so you only see the relevant panes of the debugger that have changed, and resized the window a bit, so you can see the whole call stack.

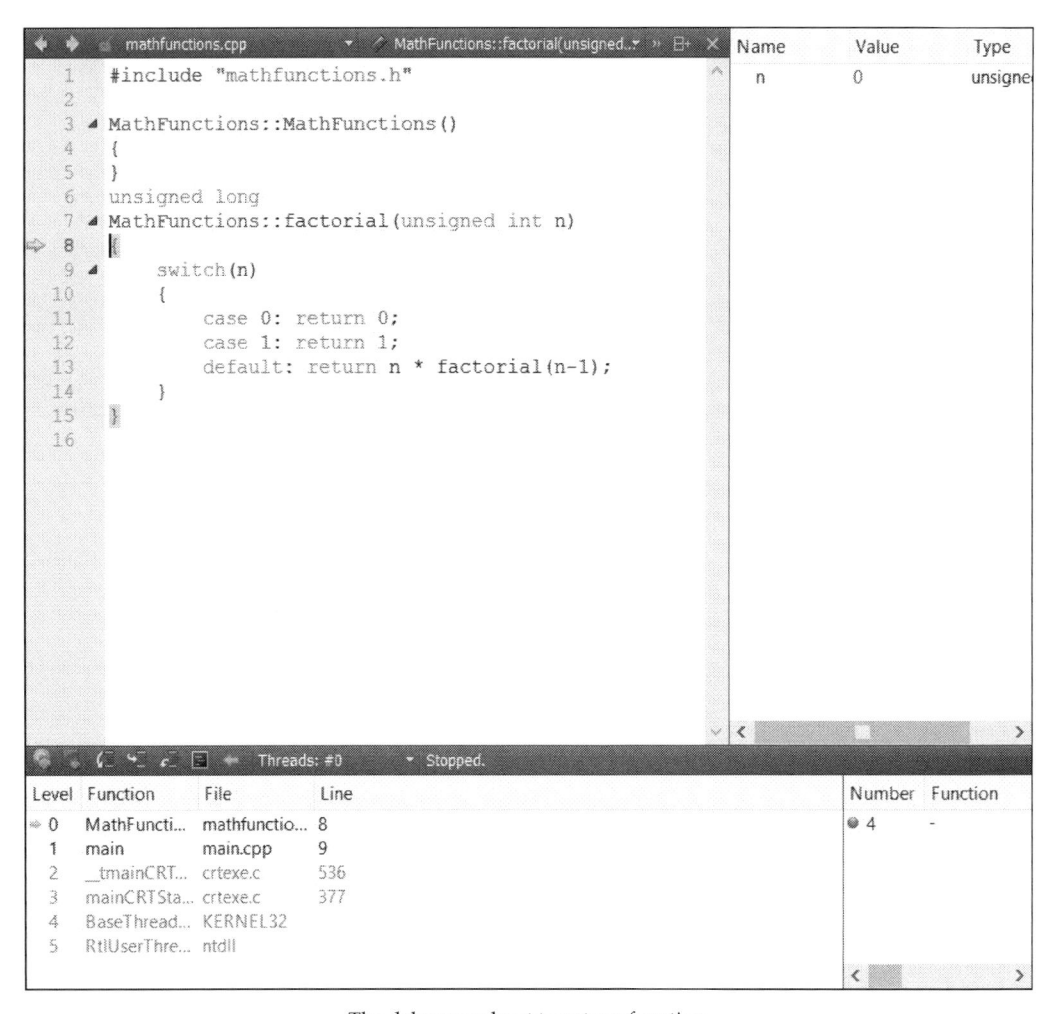

The debugger about to enter a function

At this point, if we step one more line (*F10*) again, we'll see the value for **n** change in the right-hand column, and the arrow advance to point at line **9** (again, as numbered in the screenshot). From here, we can debug my function in several ways:

- We can examine the contents of a variable by looking at it in the right-hand pane. If it's in a stack frame above the current calling frame, we can change call frames and see variables in a different call frame too.
- We can modify a variable by clicking on its value and entering a new value.
- With some debuggers, we can move the arrow to different lines in the calling function to skip one or more lines of code, or rewind the execution to re-run a segment of code over again.

This last feature—which unfortunately doesn't work with CDB—is especially powerful, because we can step through a program, observe an error, modify variables to work around the course of the error, and continue testing our code without needing to recompile our code and re-run our executable. Or, we can skip a bit of code that we know takes a while to run by substituting the new state in the variables in question and continuing from a new location in the current call frame.

There are also a number of other things we can do, from how we debug the application to various ways we can view the state of our application when it's running. On the main **Debug** menu, we can:

- Detach the debugger from a running process by choosing **Detach** from the **Debug** menu (handy if the debugger is slowing things down and we know that part of our code doesn't need to be debugged).
- Interrupt program execution, stop execution, and examine the current state by choosing **Interrupt** from the **Debug** menu (useful if our application seems caught in a long loop we weren't expecting and appears hung).
- While stopped, we can run to the line the cursor is on by choosing **Run to Line** or press *Ctrl* + *F10*.
- While stopped, we can skip to the line the cursor is on by choosing **Jump to Line**.

Fine-grained control of breakpoints

If you right-click in the breakpoint pane, you can add, edit, or delete breakpoints. Hitting **Add Breakpoint…** or **Edit Breakpoint…** brings up the Breakpoint Editor, a daunting dialog given the humble breakpoint itself. The following screenshot shows the Breakpoint Editor:

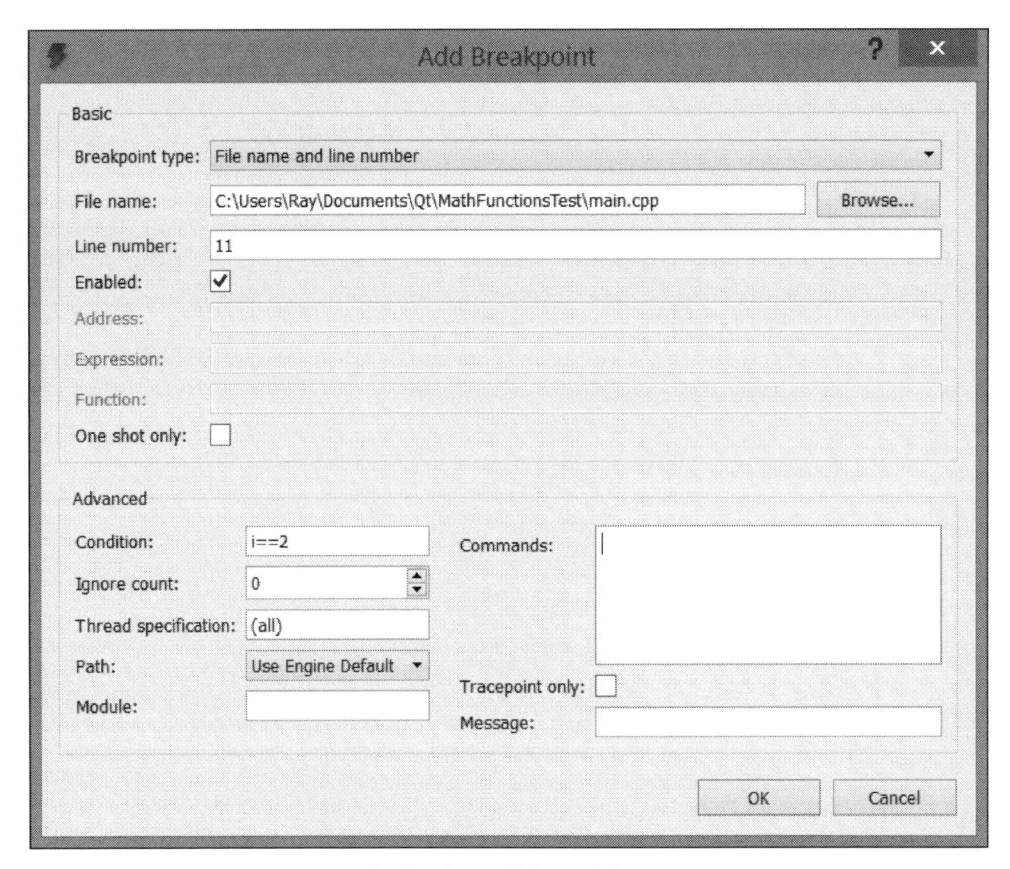

The Breakpoint Editor window

From the editor, you can fine-tune a breakpoint, setting:

- The kind of breakpoint. Most breakpoints are by filename and line number—a specific line of the code—but you have several other choices, including:
    - The entry point of a function by name
    - When a memory address is reached for execution

- When a C++ exception is thrown or caught
- When a JavaScript exception occurs
- When your main function starts
- When a new process is forked
- When a system call occurs
- When data is accessed at a fixed location, or an address indicated by an expression involving a pointer variable at runtime

- The location of the breakpoint (such as the source line number and filename, or the function), depending on your choice from the previous list.
- Whether the breakpoint is enabled or not.
- Whether the breakpoint is one-shot, that is, will be disabled after it fires once.
- Conditions for the breakpoint, such as an expression in involving program variable values, how many times to ignore the breakpoint, and which threads the breakpoint applies to.

Examining variables and memory

The variables pane shows you the values of all the variables in the current stack frame. Structures show the values of their members, so you can walk through complex data structures as well. From the variables pane, you can also copy a variable name and value to the clipboard, or just a variable value.

From the variables pane, there's a really useful feature called the **Expression Evaluator**, which lets you construct algebraic expressions about variables in your code and see the results. For example, if I'm stopped at the beginning of the `factorial` function, as you see in the *The debugger about to enter a function* screenshot, with **n** set to 6, I can right-click on the variables pane, choose **Insert New Expression Evaluator**, and type in a formula `n*(n-1)` in the dialog that appears, and a new line appears in the pane showing the expression and the value **30**. While this is a pretty contrived example, I can view pointer values and pointer dereferences as well.

I can also conditionally break execution when a variable changes; this is called a conditional breakpoint or a data breakpoint. For example, let's put a loop in our main function, and break as we execute the loop. To do this, first change `main` to read:

```
#include <QCoreApplication>
#include <QDebug>
#include "MathFunctions.h"
```

```cpp
int main(int argc, char *argv[])
{
    QCoreApplication a(argc, argv);

    int values[] = { 6, 7, 8 };

    for(int i = 0; i < sizeof(values)/sizeof(int); i++)
    {
        qDebug() << values[i]
                 << "! = "
                 << MathFunctions::factorial(values[i]);
    }

    return a.exec();
}
```

This will walk the values stored in the integer array values, and print the computed factorial of each value. Start debugging again, and let's add a data breakpoint on `i`. To do this:

1. Put a breakpoint on the first line of `main`, the line initializing `QCoreApplication`.
2. Right-click on `i` in the left pane and choose **Add Data Breakpoint at Object's Address** from the **Add Data Breakpoint** submenu.
3. Continue by pressing *F5* or the **Continue** button.

Execution will stop at line **11**, the beginning of the `for` loop, when `i` is set to `0`. Each time I hit *F5* to continue, the application runs until the value of `i` changes as a result of the `i++` statement at the end of the `for` loop.

You can also inspect and change individual values of arrays in the variable inspector, by clicking on the expansion arrow next to the array name in the variable inspector pane.

In addition to viewing and changing variable values, you can also view and change individual memory locations. You might want to do that if you're debugging a decoder or encoder for a binary format, for example, where you need to see a specific location in memory. From the variables pane, you have several choices:

- You can right-click on a given variable and open a memory window at that variable's address
- You can right-click on a given variable and open a memory window at the value that the variable points to (in other words, dereference a pointer to a memory location)

- You can right-click on the variable pane and open up a memory browser at the beginning of the current stack frame
- You can right-click on the variable pane and open up a memory browser at an arbitrary location in memory

The following screenshot shows the memory viewer showing the memory that contains the values of the array values:

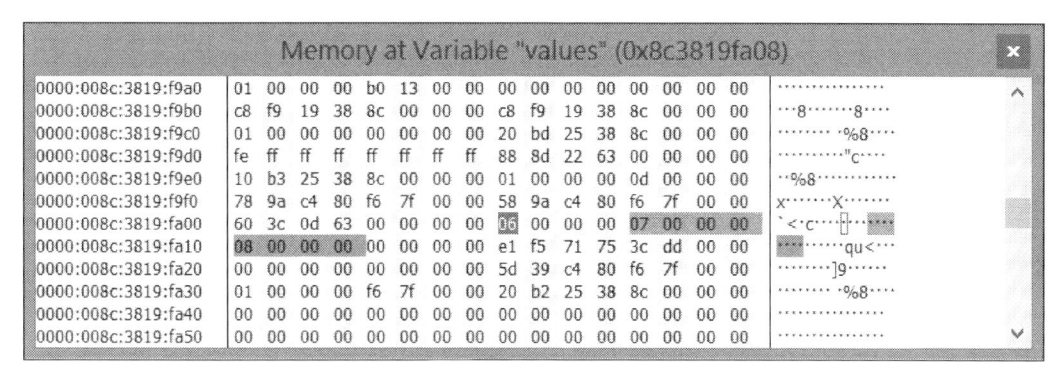

```
Memory at Variable "values" (0x8c3819fa08)
0000:008c:3819:f9a0   01 00 00 00 b0 13 00 00 00 00 00 00 00 00 00 00   ................
0000:008c:3819:f9b0   c8 f9 19 38 8c 00 00 00 c8 f9 19 38 8c 00 00 00   ...8.......8....
0000:008c:3819:f9c0   01 00 00 00 00 00 00 00 20 bd 25 38 8c 00 00 00   ........ .%8....
0000:008c:3819:f9d0   fe ff ff ff ff ff ff ff 88 8d 22 63 00 00 00 00   .........."c....
0000:008c:3819:f9e0   10 b3 25 38 8c 00 00 00 01 00 00 00 0d 00 00 00   ..%8............
0000:008c:3819:f9f0   78 9a c4 80 f6 7f 00 00 58 9a c4 80 f6 7f 00 00   x.......X.......
0000:008c:3819:fa00   60 3c 0d 63 00 00 00 00 06 00 00 00 07 00 00 00   `<.c............
0000:008c:3819:fa10   08 00 00 00 00 00 00 00 e1 f5 71 75 3c dd 00 00   ..........qu<...
0000:008c:3819:fa20   00 00 00 00 00 00 00 00 5d 39 c4 80 f6 7f 00 00   ........]9......
0000:008c:3819:fa30   01 00 00 00 f6 7f 00 00 20 b2 25 38 8c 00 00 00   ........ .%8....
0000:008c:3819:fa40   00 00 00 00 00 00 00 00 00 00 00 00 00 00 00 00   ................
0000:008c:3819:fa50   00 00 00 00 00 00 00 00 00 00 00 00 00 00 00 00   ................
```

The Memory Viewer window

The window shows the memory addresses down the left, the values of memory at sixteen bytes to a line (first in hexadecimal and then in ASCII), and colors the actual variable you've selected to open the window. You can select a range of values and then right-click to perform the following:

- Copy the values in ASCII or hexadecimal
- Set a data breakpoint on the memory location you've selected
- Transfer execution to the address you've clicked (probably not what you want to do if you're viewing the data)

Examining the call stack

The **call stack** is the hierarchy of function calls in your application execution at a point in time. Although the actual flow varies, typically in your code it begins in `main`, although what calls `main` differs from platform to platform. An obvious use for the call stack is to provide context when you press the **Interrupt** button; if your program is just off contemplating its navel in a loop somewhere, clicking on **Interrupt** and looking at the call stack can give you a clue as to what's going on.

Remember how I defined the `factorial` function in terms of itself? You can see this very clearly if you put a breakpoint in `factorial`, call it, and continue through the breakpoint a few times before looking at the call stack; you'll see something akin to the following screenshot:

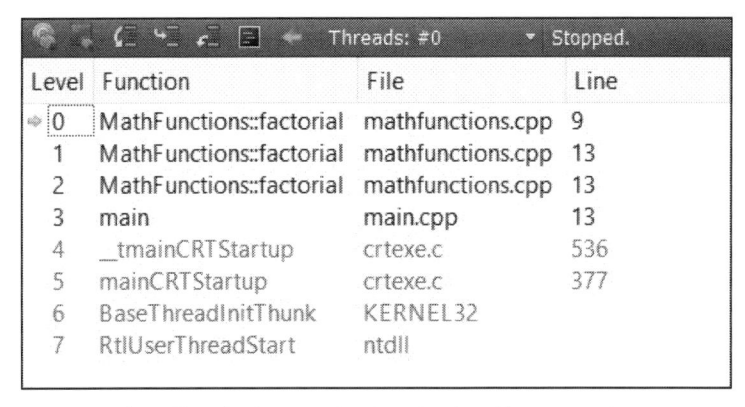

Level	Function	File	Line
0	MathFunctions::factorial	mathfunctions.cpp	9
1	MathFunctions::factorial	mathfunctions.cpp	13
2	MathFunctions::factorial	mathfunctions.cpp	13
3	main	main.cpp	13
4	__tmainCRTStartup	crtexe.c	536
5	mainCRTStartup	crtexe.c	377
6	BaseThreadInitThunk	KERNEL32	
7	RtlUserThreadStart	ntdll	

The call stack of a recursive function in mid-computation

Working from left to right, the fields of the call stack window are the stack level (numbering from the top of the stack down), the function being invoked, the file the function is defined in, and the line number of the function currently being executed. So, this stack frame says that we're on line **9** of `MathFunctions::factorial` in `mathfunctions.cpp`, called by line **13** of **MathFunctions::factorial**, which is called by line **13** of `MathFunctions::factorial` and so on, until it bottoms out in our `main` function, and the system startup code that the operating system uses to set up the application process before that.

If you right-click on a line of the call stack pane, you can:

- Reload the stack, in case the display appears corrupted.
- Copy the contents of the call stack to the clipboard; it is great for bug reports. If your application throws an exception or crashes in the debugger, you can copy the call stack and send it off to the developer responsible for that part of the code (or keep it for yourself as a souvenir).
- Open the memory editor at the address of the instruction at the line of code indicated by the function call in the call stack.
- Open the disassembler at the address of the instruction at the line of code indicated by the function call in the call stack.
- Disassemble a region of memory or the current function.
- Show the program counter address in the call stack window while debugging.

The Projects pane and building your project

You've seen how the `.pro` file affects your project's compilation, but there's even more to it than that. If you click the **Projects** button on the left of Qt Creator, you'll see the project's options, which consist of the **Build & Run** options, the **Editor** options, the **Code Style** options, and **Dependencies**, each in their own panel.

In most cases, you won't need to monkey around with any of these settings. But you may need to tinker with the **Build & Run** settings, especially if you're targeting multiple platforms, such as Windows and Linux with cross-compilers, or Android and iOS once Digia finishes support for those platforms. (I write more about this exciting development in Qt later in this book.)

The final thing you should know about is the build and run kit selector. Qt is one of the best cross-platform toolkits available today, and you can easily find yourself working on a system supporting multiple platforms, such as Linux and Android, or multiple versions of Qt. To support this, Qt has the notion of a build kit, which is just the headers, libraries, and associated stuff to support a specific platform. You can install multiple build kits, and choose which build kit you're compiling against by choosing **Open Build** and **Run Kit Selector.....** By default, if you followed the steps in the previous chapter to install Qt Creator, you'll have one build kit installed; from the Digia site, you can choose others. In a later chapter, we'll build a sample application for Qt on Android. To do this, you'd need to download and install the Qt on Android build kit, and then tell Qt Creator about the new kit. Adding kits is easy, you just need to install the kit using your operating system, and then do the following in Qt Creator:

1. Click on **Projects** on the left.
2. Click on **Manage Kits...** on the upper left-hand side of the pane that appears. The **Build & Run** options window appears.
3. Qt may autodetect your new kit, or you may need to add it by clicking on **Add**. Once you click on **Add**, you'll need to specify the target platform (such as an Android device), the compiler to use, and so forth.

For the build settings, there are configuration options for your release and debug builds. In the **Build Settings** editor, you can control whether the build products are placed in their own directory (the default, a so-called shadow build where your build outputs are mixed with the source code), the `qmake` configuration for the build (and actually see how Qt Creator will invoke `qmake`), how Qt Creator cleans your project, and any environment variables you need to set for the build.

The run settings let you control whether your application runs locally or is deployed on a remote host (not always supported, but usually the case for platforms such as Android), any command-line arguments you want to pass to your applications, and the settings for the performance analyzer tool, which I will talk more about in *Chapter 4*, *Localizing Your Application with Qt Linguist*.

In the **Editor** panel, you can set specific editor options for this project. These override the global Qt Creator defaults, which you can set by choosing **Options** from the **Tools** menu and selecting the **Text Editor** option. These options include details like whether to use tabs or spaces when formatting your code (I strongly suggest you use spaces; it's compatible with editors everywhere), the number of spaces per tab stop, whether or not automatic indentation occurs, how source files should be encoded, and so forth.

The **Code Style** panel is another override to the global settings for Qt Creator (this time, it's the C++ and Qt Quick panels of the **Options** dialog available from the **Options** menu). Here, you can pick default styles, or edit the styles.

> I'd strongly recommend that you pick a style that matches the existing source code you're editing; if you're starting from a blank page, the Qt default style is quite readable, and is my favorite.

The **Dependencies** panel lets you set the build order if your project file contains multiple subprojects, so that things build in the right order. For example, we could choose to open both our library project and our test project; if we do, we'll see the `MathFunctions` library listed in the dependencies, and we can select that project to build before the test application is built.

A review – running and debugging your application

You'll spend a lot of time editing, compiling, and debugging your code in Qt Creator, so, it's wise to remember the following basics:

- The arrow key runs your application without the debugger; to debug your application, choose the arrow key with the bug icon on it.
- You can switch between the editor view and the debug view of your application by clicking on the **Edit** or **Debug** view choice on the left; if you debug your application, Qt Creator will enter the debug view automatically.

- There's more to breakpoints than just stopping at a line of code! Use data breakpoints to help pin down weird bugs that happen only sometimes, or to quickly skip over the first bazillion items of a large loop.
- The variable pane lets you see more than just the contents of variables; you can also add expressions composed of several variables and arithmetic, or view arbitrary memory locations.
- Want to hack around a bug during a debugging session? You can change the values of variables in the variable pane and continue running, changing the program state as you go.

Summary

Qt Creator's integrated development environment contains an editor and tools to start the compiler, linker, and debugger to build and debug your applications. Using it, you can start and stop your application, place breakpoints while your application is stopped, or examine variables or the logical flow of your application.

While Qt Creator manages most of a project for you, sometimes you just have to get down and dirty with a `.pro` file. You can use scopes to handle conditional compilation (things like when building for a specific platform, or whether a file should be included in release or debug mode). The `.pro` file consists of scopes, variables, and their values; by setting the variables that the `.pro` file feeds `qmake`, `qmake` understands the dependencies in your project and magically creates a Make file to build your application.

In the next chapter, we'll turn from the mechanics of making a project build and look at Qt Creator's UI designer, and give you a brief introduction into the worlds of both Qt Widgets and Qt Quick.

3
Designing Your Application with Qt Designer

Qt is perhaps best known as a cross-platform user interface toolkit, and only in the last few years has Qt Creator really evolved to be a full software development environment. Even in its early releases, however, Qt had an excellent facility for building user interfaces with Qt Designer, now part of Qt Creator. More recently, the developers building Qt have added Qt Quick as a second option for user interface development. Qt Quick extends the Qt libraries and the Qt Designer capabilities of Qt Creator to build fluid interfaces for touchscreens and set-top boxes and to facilitate the declarative nature of Qt Quick and **Qt Meta-object Language** (**QML**).

In this chapter, we will learn how to create user interfaces using Qt Designer, the user interface builder in Qt Creator. We begin by introducing key concepts to understanding the Qt framework: **signals** and **slots**. Next, we revisit using Qt Designer to create application forms, the basis of your user interface when using Qt Widgets. We touch on how to add resources and access them in your application, an important facet of user interface design. Then, we return to the code for a bit and build on the fundamentals of QML you learned in *Chapter 1, Getting Started with Qt Creator*. At the end of this chapter, you'll be well equipped to decide whether your application should be written using Qt GUI or Qt Quick, and to build your application with the help of the documentation that accompanies Qt Creator.

Code interlude – signals and slots

In software systems, there is often the need to couple different objects. Ideally, this coupling should be loose, that is, not dependent on the system's compile-time configuration. This is especially obvious when you consider user interfaces; for example, a button press may adjust the contents of a text widget or cause something to appear or disappear. Many systems use events for this purpose; components offering data encapsulate that data in an event, and an event loop (or, more recently, an event listener) catches the event and performs some action.

Qt offers a better way: signals and slots. Like an event, the sending component generates a signal—in Qt parlance, the object emits a signal—which recipient objects may receive in a slot for the purpose. Qt objects may emit more than one signal, and signals may carry arguments; in addition, multiple Qt objects can have slots connected to the same signal, making it easy to arrange one-to-many notifications. Equally important, if no object is interested in a signal, it can be safely ignored, and no slots connected to the signal. Any object that inherits from `QObject`, Qt's base class for objects, can emit signals or provide slots for connection to signals. Under the hood, Qt provides extensions to C++ syntax for declaring signals and slots.

A simple example will help make this clear. The classic example you find in the Qt documentation is an excellent one, and we'll use it again it here, with some extension's. Imagine you have the need for a counter, that is, a container that holds an integer. In C++, you might write:

```
class Counter
{
public:
  Counter() { m_value = 0; }
  int value() const { return m_value; }
  void setValue(int value);

private:
  int m_value;
};
```

The `Counter` class has a single private member, `m_value`, bearing its value. Clients can invoke the value to obtain the counter's value, or set its value by invoking `setValue` with a new value.

In Qt, using signals and slots, we write the class this way:

```
#include <QObject>
class Counter : public QObject
{
  Q_OBJECT
public:
  Counter() { m_value = 0; }
  int value() const { return m_value; }
   public slots:
  void setValue(int value);
  void increment();
  void decrement();
signals:
  void valueChanged(int newValue);
private:
  int m_value;
};
```

This `Counter` class inherits from `QObject`, the base class for all Qt objects. All `QObject` subclasses must include the declaration `Q_OBJECT` as the first element of their definition; this macro expands to Qt code implementing the subclass-specific glue necessary for the Qt object and signal-slot mechanism. The constructor remains the same, initializing our private member to zero. Similarly, the accessor method value remains the same, returning the current value for the counter.

An object's slots must be public, and are declared using the Qt extension to C++ public slots. This code defines three slots: a `setValue` slot, which accepts a new value for the counter, and the `increment` and `decrement` slots, which increment and decrement the value of the counter. Slots may take arguments, but do not return them; the communication between a signal and its slots is one way, initiating with the signal and terminating with the slot(s) connected to the signal.

The counter offers a single signal. Like slots, signals are also declared using a Qt extension to C++, `signals`. In the example above, a `Counter` object emits the signal `valueChanged` with a single argument, which is the new value of the counter. A signal is a function signature, not a method; Qt's extensions to C++ use the type signature of signals and slots to ensure type safety between signal-slot connections, a key advantage signals and slots have over other decoupled messaging schemes.

As the developers, it's our responsibility to implement each slot in our class with whatever application logic makes sense. The `Counter` class's slots look like this:

```
void Counter::setValue(int newValue)
{
  if (newValue != m_value) {
      m_value = newValue;
      emit valueChanged(newValue);
  }
}

void Counter::increment()
{
  setValue(value() + 1);
}

void Counter::decrement()
{
  setValue(value() - 1);
}
```

We use the implementation of the `setValue` slot as a method, which is what all slots are at their heart. The `setValue` slot takes a new value and assigns the new value to the `Counter` class's private member variable if they aren't the same. Then, the signal emits the `valueChanged` signal, using the Qt extension `emit`, which triggers an invocation to the slots connected to the signal.

> This is a common pattern for signals that handle object properties: testing the property to be set for equality with the new value, and only assigning and emitting a signal if the values are unequal.

If we had a button, say `QPushButton`, we could connect its clicked signal to the `increment` or `decrement` slot, so that a click on the button incremented or decremented the counter. I'd do that using the `QObject::connect` method, like this:

```
QPushButton* button = new QPushButton(tr("Increment"), this);
Counter* counter = new Counter(this);
QObject::connect(button, SIGNAL(clicked(void)),
                 Counter, SLOT(increment(void)));
```

We first create the `QPushButton` and `Counter` objects. The `QPushButton` constructor takes a string, the label for the button, which we denote to be the string `Increment` or its localized counterpart.

Why do we pass this to each constructor? Qt provides a parent-child memory management between QObjects and their descendants, easing clean-up when you're done using an object. When you free an object, Qt also frees any children of the parent object, so you don't have to. The parent-child relationship is set at construction time; I'm signaling to the constructors that when the object invoking this code is freed, the push button and counter may be freed as well. (Of course, the invoking method must also be a subclass of `QObject` for this to work.)

Next, I call `QObject::connect`, passing first the source object and the signal to be connected, and then the receiver object and the slot to which the signal should be sent. The types of the signal and the slot must match, and the signals and slots must be wrapped in the `SIGNAL` and `SLOT` macros, respectively.

Signals can also be connected to signals, and when that happens, the signals are chained and trigger any slots connected to the downstream signals. For example, I could write:

```
Counter a, b;
QObject::connect(&a, SIGNAL(valueChanged(int)),
                 &b, SLOT(setValue(int)));
```

This connects the counter b with the counter a, so that any change in value to the counter a also changes the value of the counter b.

Signals and slots are used throughout Qt, both for user interface elements and to handle asynchronous operations, such as the presence of data on network sockets and HTTP transaction results. Under the hood, signals and slots are very efficient, boiling down to function dispatch operations, so you shouldn't hesitate to use the abstraction in your own designs. Qt provides a special build tool, the meta-object compiler, which compiles the extensions to C++ that signals and slots require and generates the additional code necessary to implement the mechanism.

Creating forms in Qt Designer

Let's create a simple calculator application using Qt Designer and two forms: one form taking the arguments for an arithmetic operation, and a second dialog form for presenting the results. I'll do this twice in this chapter, first showing you how to do this using Qt GUI, and again using Qt Quick. The example is contrived, but will show you how to create multiple user interface forms in both environments, and give you practice in working with signals and slots.

Designing Your Application with Qt Designer

Creating the main form

In *Chapter 1*, *Getting Started with Qt Creator*, you learned the basic elements of the Qt GUI Designer, including the palette of widgets you can use, the central edit pane, the tree of objects, and the property view. The following screenshot shows the Qt Designer again:

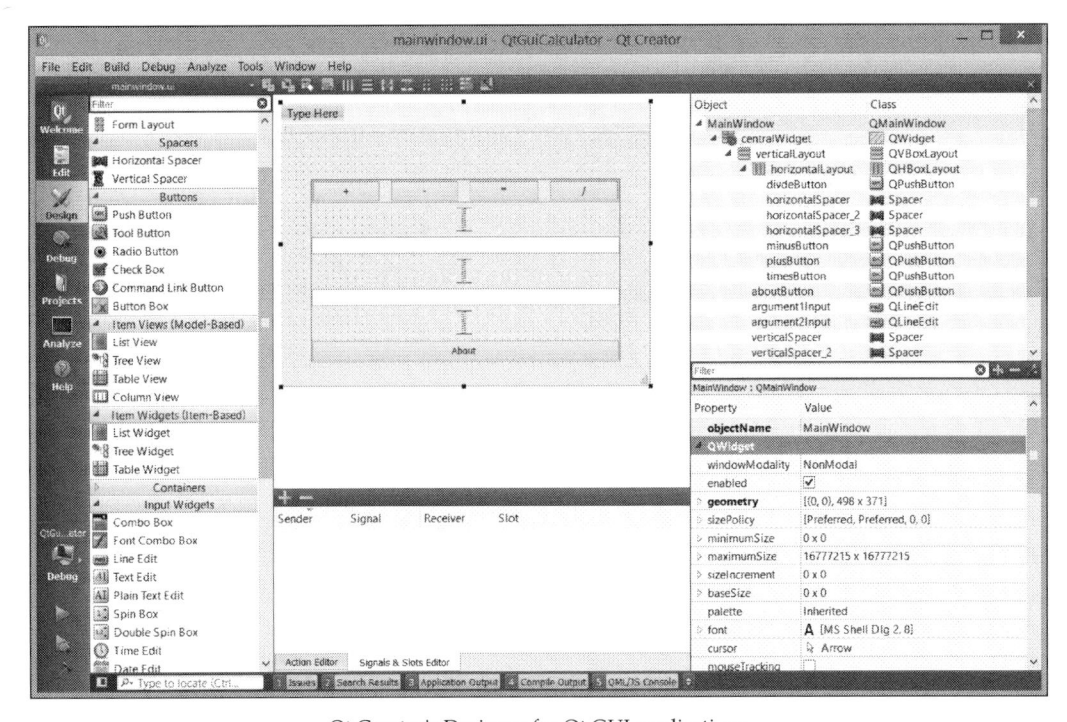

Qt Creator's Designer for Qt GUI applications

Working from left to right, the parts of the screen you see are:

- The views selector, presently indicating that the Qt Designer view is active
- The palette of possible widgets you can lay out on your form
- The form editor, above the connection editor, which lets you wire signals and slots between widgets
- The object tree, indicating all of the objects that have been laid out on the form and showing their parent-child relationships through the use of nested lists
- Below the object tree is the property editor, where you can edit the compile-time properties of any item you select on the form editor

Chapter 3

Let's begin by creating a new Qt GUI project (select **Qt Gui Application** from the **New File or Projects...** dialog) naming the project `QtGuiCalculator`, and then follow these steps:

1. In the **Forms** folder of the project, double-click on the `mainwindow.ui` file. The designer will open.
2. Drag out **Vertical Layout** from the palette.
3. Right-click on the layout and choose **Lay out**, then choose **Adjust Size**. The layout will shrink to a point.
4. Drag two **Line Edit** widgets and drop them on the vertical layout in the object viewer (the far-right pane). You'll see the vertical layout grow to accept each of the line editors. You should now have something that looks like the following screenshot:

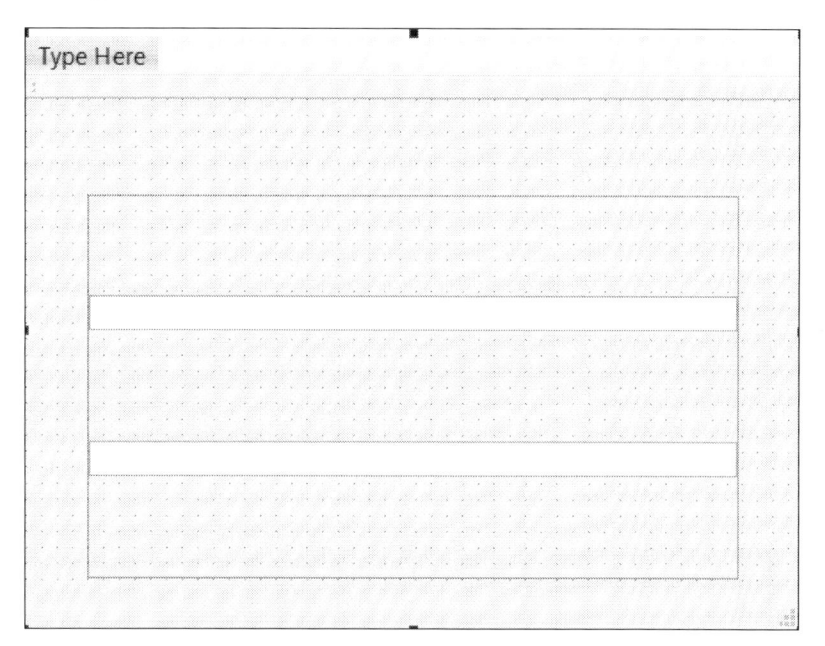

Your layout after the first two text fields

5. Drag the **Horizontal Layout** and drop it on the vertical layout in the object viewer.
6. Drag-and-drop four **Push Button** widgets on the horizontal layout you just added.
7. Resize the containing window so that the entire layout is shown in the window.

8. Rename the buttons `plusButton`, `minusButton`, `timesButton`, and `divideButton` using the property browser in the lower-right corner. As you do so, scroll down to the **text** property (under **QAbstractButton**) and give each button a logical label like +, -, *, and /.
9. Select the top input line and name it `argument1Input`.
10. Select the bottom input line and name it `argument2Input`.

The next screenshot shows what you should see in the Qt Designer form editor pane so far. You can also manually arrange the buttons by breaking the layout and positioning them using the mouse, but that typically makes your layout less robust to window resizing, and is generally not a good idea:

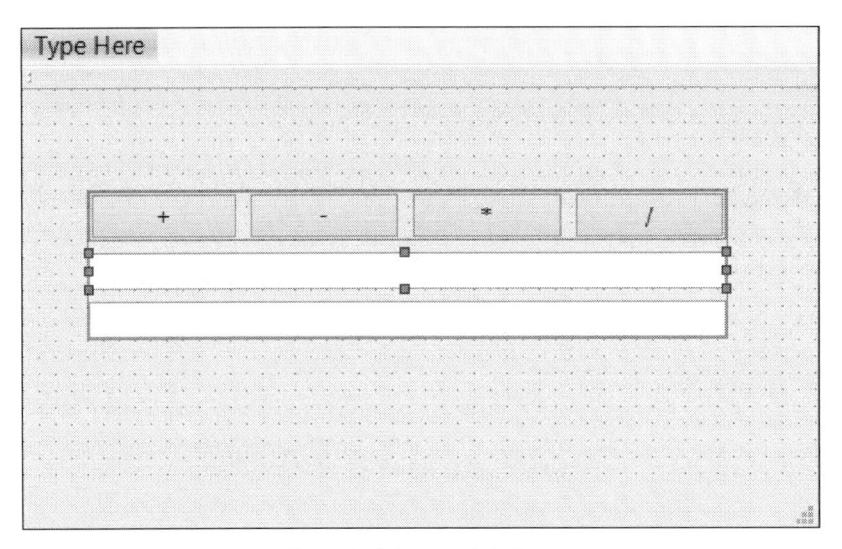

Our calculator user interface

So far, this is pretty straightforward. We used a vertical layout and a horizontal layout to lay out the various controls; this takes advantage of Qt's dynamic constraints on widget layout and sizing. All widgets have a minimum and a maximum size, which are used by layouts to determine the actual size a widget consumes. Some widgets are elastic; that is, they stretch to fill their contents. When specifying the actual size of a widget, you can specify that it takes one of the following values in each of the x and y axes:

- The minimum size of the widget
- The maximum size of the widget

- A fixed size between its minimum and maximum
- An expanding size, expanding to fit the contents of the widget

Qt provides four kinds of layouts, which you can mix and match as we just did. You've encountered the vertical and horizontal layouts; there's also a grid layout, which lets you organize things in an *m* × *n* grid, and a form layout, which organizes widgets in a manner similar to how the native platform enumerates fields on a form.

Right now, our layout's a little bunched up. Let's add some spacers to better fill the space in the window, and also add a button for an about box:

1. Drag **Vertical Spacer** and drop it between the input lines, and a second vertical spacer between the horizontal layout containing the row of buttons and the input line.
2. Drag a **Tool Button** widget to the vertical layout, and add a spacer between the bottom line and the push button.
3. Name the last push button `aboutButton` and give it the text `About`. We'll add an icon later.

The following screenshot shows the application as we've constructed it in the designer if you press the **Run** button:

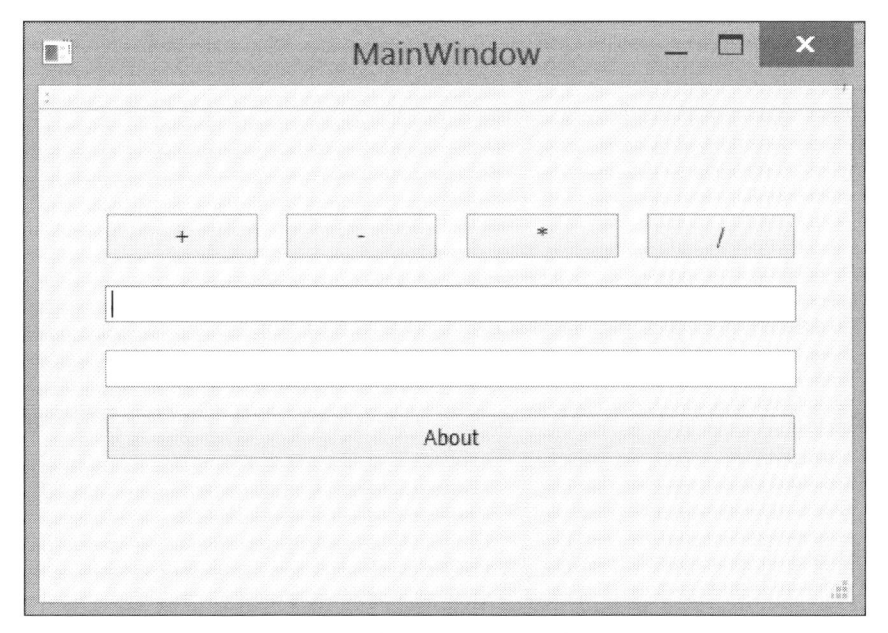

Our application's main window

Now, let's make our result dialog. Right-click on the project and choose **Add New…**, then:

1. In the dialog that appears, choose **Qt** on the left, and then **Qt Designer Form** in the middle. Click on **Choose**.
2. Choose a dialog style for your dialog; choose **Dialog with Buttons Bottom** and click on **Next**.
3. Name the file resultdialog.ui and click on **Next**.
4. Click on **Finish**.
5. In the dialog that appears, drag out **Form Layout**. Right-click on it and choose **Lay out** and **Adjust size**.
6. Add a **Label** widget to the form layout. Change its text to read Result.
7. Drag out another label, and name it result.

Now may be a good time for you to experiment with layouts and spacers, and style the dialog any way you wish.

Using application resources

Now, let's add an icon to the application for the **About** button. You can draw one, or go to a website such as The *Noun Project* (http://bit.ly/16n9bOk) for a suitable icon. Icons can be PNG, JPEG, or other formats; a good choice is SVG, because SVG images are vector based and scale correctly to different sizes. Put the resource file in your project directory, and then:

1. Choose the **Edit** view in Qt Creator.
2. Right-click on the solution and click on **Add New…**; then, choose **Qt** and **Qt Resource File**.
3. Name the file resources.
4. Add it to the current project.
5. If resources.qrc isn't already open in the editor, double-click on it in the solution pane. The resource file editor will appear.
6. Click on **Add**, choose **Add prefix**, and prefix /.
7. Click on **Add** again, select **Add Files**, and choose your icon.

Icons are loaded in the read-only segment of your application through the Qt resource compiler. You can access them anywhere you'd access a file by prefixing the path and name of the resource with a colon. For example, we might place a text file in our application resources and then open the file for reading, like this:

```
QFile file(":/data/myfile.txt");
file.open(QIODevice::ReadOnly | QIODevice::Text);

while (!file.atEnd()) {
  QByteArray line = file.readLine();
  process_line(line);
}
```

Application resources are suitable for text and small media files such as icons or images. You should avoid using them for larger items like movies and large sounds, however, because they'll needlessly bloat the size of your application binary. For those purposes, it's better to package media files with your application and load them directly from the disk.

In the next section, we'll use the resource you added, when we add our about box to the application.

Instantiating forms, message boxes, and dialogs in your application

The Qt Designer generates an XML-based layout file (which ends in .ui) for each form you create in the designer. At compile time, Qt Creator compiles the layout into a header file that constructs the components for your user interface layout. The pattern typically used by Qt applications is to construct a private layout class that is instantiated by a main window or dialog's constructor, and then the user interface is instantiated. Here's how it works for the main window:

```
#ifndef MAINWINDOW_H
#define MAINWINDOW_H

#include <QMainWindow>

namespace Ui {
  class MainWindow;
}
```

Designing Your Application with Qt Designer

```
class ResultDialog;

class MainWindow : public QMainWindow
{
    Q_OBJECT

public:
    explicit MainWindow(QWidget *parent = 0);
    ~MainWindow();

private:
    Ui::MainWindow *ui;
};

#endif // MAINWINDOW_H

// In mainwindow.cpp:
#include "mainwindow.h"

// mainwindow.cpp
#include "ui_mainwindow.h"

MainWindow::MainWindow(QWidget *parent) :
    QMainWindow(parent),
    ui(new Ui::MainWindow),
{
    ui->setupUi(this);
}
```

The `Ui::MainWindow` class is automatically constructed by the Qt Designer; by including its declaration in `mainwindow.cpp`, we create an instance of it and assign that instance to the `ui` field. Once initialized, we call its `setupUi` function, which creates the entire user interface you sketched out in Qt Designer.

The controls we laid out in Qt Designer are accessible as field names. For example, we can modify `mainwindow.cpp` to invoke an about box by adding a slot to `mainwindow.h` to handle the case when you click on the **About** button, and then add the code to invoke an about box in the implementation of the slot. To do that, follow these steps:

1. Add a `public slots` declaration to `mainwindow.h`, along with a slot named `aboutClicked`. It should now read:

```
class MainWindow : public QMainWindow
{
    Q_OBJECT

public:
    explicit MainWindow(QWidget *parent = 0);
    ~MainWindow();

public slots:
    void aboutClicked();

private:
    Ui::MainWindow *ui;
};
```

2. Add the implementation of the `aboutClicked` slot to `mainwindow.cpp`. This code constructs a `QMessageBox` object on the stack, and sets its icon to the icon you added in your resources earlier, the text of the dialog to `"Lorem ipsum"`, and the title of the message box to `"About"`. The `exec` method of the `QMessageBox` invocation opens the message box and blocks the application flow until you dismiss the message box. It should read:

```
void MainWindow::aboutClicked()
{
    QMessageBox messageBox;
    messageBox.setIconPixmap(QPixmap(":/icon.png"));
    messageBox.setText("Lorem ipsum.");
    messageBox.setWindowTitle("About");
    messageBox.exec();
}
```

3. At the top of `mainwindow.cpp`, add an `include` statement for the `QMessageBox` class:

```
#include <QMessageBox>
```

4. In the `MainWindow` constructor, connect the signal from the about button to the slot you just created. Your constructor should now read:

```
MainWindow::MainWindow(QWidget *parent) :
    QMainWindow(parent),
    ui(new Ui::MainWindow),
    results(0)
```

[57]

```
    {
        ui->setupUi(this);
        QObject::connect(ui->aboutButton, SIGNAL(clicked()),
                         this, SLOT(aboutClicked()));
    }
```

If we build the application, we now have a fully functioning about box, including the application icon you chose. The `connect` call is just like the previous signal-slot connections we've seen; it connects the `clicked` signal of `aboutButton` to your `aboutClicked` slot in the main window UI.

A word on naming signals and slots before we continue: a signal is typically named a verb in its past tense, denoting the semantics of the event that just occurred that it's trying to signal. A slot should somehow match those semantics, preferably including more detail as to how the signal is being handled. So Qt names the button's `clicked` signal logically, and I expand on this by giving a slot named `aboutClicked`. Of course, you can name your signals and slots whatever you like, but this is a good practice to follow.

Before we wire up the other buttons and implement our calculator logic, we need to set up the class for our `results` dialog. We'll follow the pattern of the `MainWindow` class, creating a private `ui` member that contains an instance of the compile-time generated object that constructs the UI for the results dialog. You can create the `ResultDialog` class using the **New File** wizard available by right-clicking on the project; choose **Qt Designer Form Class** and name it `ResultDialog`. The class itself should inherit from `QDialog`. The header file should look like this:

```
#ifndef RESULTDIALOG_H
#define RESULTDIALOG_H

#include <QDialog>

namespace Ui {
    class Dialog;
}
class ResultDialog : public QDialog
{
    Q_OBJECT
public:
    explicit ResultDialog(QWidget *parent = 0);
    ~ResultDialog();
```

```
private:
    Ui::Dialog *ui;

};

#endif // RESULTDIALOG_H
```

The first thing we need to do is forward-declare the `Dialog` class created by the Qt Designer; we do this in the namespace `Ui`, so it doesn't conflict with any other code in my application. Then, we need to declare a pointer to an instance of that class as a private member variable; we name this pointer `ui`, as was done for the `MainWindow` class.

You can guess what our `ResultDialog` implementation looks like:

```
#include "resultdialog.h"
#include "ui_resultdialog.h"

ResultDialog::ResultDialog(QWidget *parent) :
    QDialog(parent),
    ui(new Ui::Dialog)
{
    ui->setupUi(this);
}

ResultDialog::~ResultDialog()
{
    delete ui;
}
```

At construction time, it makes an instance of our `Ui:Dialog` class, and then invokes its `setupUi` method to create an instance of the user interface at runtime.

Wiring the Qt GUI application logic

The application logic for the calculator is simple: we add a property setter to the `ResultDialog` implementation that lets us set the `result` field of the dialog, and then wire up some arithmetic, signals, and slots in `MainWindow` to do the actual computation and show the dialog.

First, the change to `ResultDialog`:

```
void ResultDialog::setResult(float r)
{
    ui->result->setText(QString::number(r));
}
```

This method takes a float, the value to show in the dialog, and formats the result as a string using Qt's default formatting. Qt is fully internationalized; if you do this in English-speaking locales, it will use a decimal point, while if you do it with a locale set to a region where a comma is used as the decimal separator, it will use a comma instead. The `number` method is a handy one, with overloads taking doubles and floats, as well as integers, and arguments to indicate the precision and exponentiation of the returned string.

Now, the modified `MainWindow` class. First, the revised class declaration:

```
#ifndef MAINWINDOW_H
#define MAINWINDOW_H

#include <QMainWindow>
#include <QPair>

namespace Ui {
    class MainWindow;
}
class ResultDialog;

class MainWindow : public QMainWindow
{
    Q_OBJECT

    typedef QPair<float, float> Arguments;
public:
    explicit MainWindow(QWidget *parent = 0);
    ~MainWindow();

    Arguments arguments();
signals:
    void computed(float f);
public slots:
    void aboutClicked();
    void plusClicked();
    void minusClicked();
    void timesClicked();
    void divideClicked();
    void showResult(float r);
```

```
    private:
        Ui::MainWindow *ui;
        ResultDialog* results;
    };

    #endif // MAINWINDOW_H
```

In addition to the base class QMainWindow, I now include QPair, a simple Qt template that lets us pass pairs of values. We'll use the QPair template, type-defined as Arguments, to pass around the pair of arguments for an arithmetic operation.

I add a signal, computed, which the class triggers any time it performs an arithmetic operation. I also add slots for each of the arithmetic button clicks: plusClicked, minusClicked, timesClicked, and dividedClicked. Finally, I add a signal showResult, which shows the result when a computation occurs.

The constructor of MainWindow now needs to do a bunch of signal-slot wiring for all of our buttons, signals, and slots:

```
    MainWindow::MainWindow(QWidget *parent) :
        QMainWindow(parent),
        ui(new Ui::MainWindow),
        results(0)
    {
        ui->setupUi(this);
        QObject::connect(ui->aboutButton, SIGNAL(clicked()),
                         this, SLOT(aboutClicked()));
        QObject::connect(this, SIGNAL(computed(float)),
                         this, SLOT(showResult(float)));
        QObject::connect(ui->plusButton, SIGNAL(clicked()),
                         this, SLOT(plusClicked()));
        QObject::connect(ui->minusButton, SIGNAL(clicked()),
                         this, SLOT(minusClicked()));
        QObject::connect(ui->timesButton, SIGNAL(clicked()),
                         this, SLOT(timesClicked()));
        QObject::connect(ui->divdeButton, SIGNAL(clicked()),
                         this, SLOT(divideClicked()));
    }
```

After connecting the about button to the slot that shows the about dialog, I next connect the computed signal from MainWindow to its showResult slot. Note that this signal/slot carries an argument, the value to show. The remaining four connections connect each of the operation buttons with the code to perform a specific arithmetic operation.

The `showResult` slot creates a new `ResultDialog` object if we don't already have one, sets its result to the incoming value, and invokes the dialog:

```
void MainWindow::showResult(float r)
{
    if (!results)
    {
        results = new ResultDialog();
    }
    results->setResult(r);
    results->exec();
}
```

The `arguments` method is a helper method used by each of the arithmetic functions, it fetches the values from each of the input lines, converts them from strings to floating-point numbers, and does a little bit of error checking to ensure that the entries are valid floating-point numbers:

```
MainWindow::Arguments MainWindow::arguments()
{
    bool ok1, ok2;
    float a1 = ui->argument1Input->text().toFloat(&ok1);
    float a2 = ui->argument2Input->text().toFloat(&ok2);
    if (!ok1 || !ok2)
    {
        QMessageBox messageBox;
        messageBox.setIconPixmap(QPixmap(":/icon.png"));
        messageBox.setText("One of your entries is not a valid
                          number.");
        messageBox.setWindowTitle("Error");
        messageBox.exec();
    }
    return Arguments(a1, a2);
}
```

The `QString` method `toFloat` does just that: it converts a string to a floating-point number, returns the number, and sets the Boolean passed in to `true` if the conversion was successful, and `false` otherwise. The code does this for both argument input lines, then checks the resulting Boolean values, and reports an error if either argument is malformed, before returning a QPair of the arguments to the caller.

The remaining code actually performs the arithmetic, signaling that a computation has occurred when the operation is complete. For example, take the `plusClicked` slot:

```
void MainWindow::plusClicked()
{
    Arguments a = arguments();
    emit computed(a.first + a.second);
}
```

This obtains the arguments from the input lines using the `arguments` function, computes the sum, and then emits the computed signal with the summed value. Because we connected the computed signal to the `showResults` slot, this triggers a call to `showResults`, which creates the `ResultDialog` object if necessary, and shows the dialog with the computed result. The `minusClicked`, `timesClicked`, and `divideClicked` methods are all similar.

Learning more about Qt GUI widgets

There are whole books written about programming with the Qt GUI widget set: it's a very rich widget set that includes just about everything you'd need to build the average Macintosh, Windows, or Linux application, and has the advantage that the UI controls are familiar to most computer users. To explore further, see the Qt documentation at `http://bit.ly/17stfw3`.

Code interlude – Qt Quick and QML syntax

Most of the programming you do at the lowest level is imperative: you describe how an algorithm should work ("take this value and square it", "search for the first occurrence of this string and replace it", "format this data this way", and so forth). With Qt Quick, your programming is largely declarative: instead of saying *how*, you say *what*. For example, in C++ with Qt, we might write code like this to draw a rectangle:

```
QRect r(0, 0, 16, 16);
QPainter p;
p.setBrush(QBrush(Qt::blue));
p.drawRect(r);
```

Designing Your Application with Qt Designer

This code creates a 16 x 16 pixel rectangle, allocates a `QPainter` object that does the drawing, tells the painter that its brush should be colored blue, and then tells the painter to draw the rectangle. In QML, I'd simply write the rectangle:

```
import QtQuick 2.0
Rectangle {
    width: 16
    height: 16
    color: "blue"
}
```

The difference is obvious: I am just saying that there is a blue rectangle that's 16 x 16 pixels. It's up to the Qt Quick runtime to determine how to draw the rectangle.

Qt Quick's underlying language is QML. It is based heavily on JavaScript, and in fact, most things that you can write in JavaScript you can also express in QML. Expression syntax is essentially unchanged: assignments, arithmetic, and so forth are all the same, and the name-value system is functionally the same, although object frames may be preceded by a type declaration (as you see with the `Rectangle` example that I just showed you).

> A key exception to the "what works in JavaScript works in QML" rule is the lack of a document object model (DOM) and things like the document root for global variables because there's no root context or DOM on which other things hang. If you're porting a web application to QML, be prepared to refactor those parts of your application's architecture.

Objects in QML must be parented in the fashion of a tree; each QML file must contain an encapsulating object, and then can have child objects that have child objects. However, there must be a single root for the hierarchy at the top of the file. Often, this root is a rectangle, which draws a base rectangle on which its children are presented, or an item, which is a container for a more complex user interface element that doesn't actually draw anything. Each item may have a name, which is stored in its `id` property.

Most visible QML items can have states; that is, a collection of properties that apply when a particular state is active. This lets you do things such as declare the difference between a button's dormant and pressed state; pressing the button just toggles between the states, and the button's color, shadow, and so on can all change with you, and there is no need to change each individual property.

A key concept in QML that's not present in JavaScript is that of **binding**: if two QML object properties share the same value, changing one changes the other. Binding couples values with notifications about values is similar to how references work in C++, or how pass-by reference works in other languages, but this happens in QML at the level of the variable name being referenced. This is very handy in coding things such as animations, because you can use the value of one object as the value for another object, and when the underlying value changes in one place, both objects are updated.

QML files can depend on each other, or include files of JavaScript for business logic. You've already seen one example of this at the top of every QML file: the `import` directive instructs the runtime to include the indicated file and version, so when I write `import QtQuick 2.0`, the runtime finds the declaration of the QtQuick module Version 2.0 and includes its symbols when parsing the file. This is how you can encapsulate functionality. QML files in your project are included by default, while you can also include JavaScript files and assign them to a specific JavaScript variable. For example, we could have a JavaScript file `calculatorLogic.js` that implements all of the functionality of my calculator, and in the QML, write:

```
import QtQuick 2.0
import "calculatorLogic.js" as CalculatorLogic
Item {
  // someplace in code
  CalculatorLogic.add(argument1, argument2);
}
```

The initial import loads JavaScript and assigns its value to the QML object `CalculatorLogic`; I can then dispatch methods and access properties of that object as if it were any other QML object.

Qt Quick declares a number of basic datatypes; these match closely with the datatypes you find in Qt when writing C++ code, although the syntax can differ. Some of the most important types you'll encounter are:

- A point with the `x` and `y` properties
- A rectangle with the `x`, `y`, `width`, and `height` properties
- A size with the `width` and `height` properties
- A color, which is a quoted string in HTML RGB notation or a named color from Qt's lexicon of colors (most colors you can think of have names in QML)

- A 2D, 3D, or 4D vector
- Basic types including Boolean values, strings, integers, and floating-point numbers

There are also a lot of visible types for user interface construction; in this chapter, there's only room to touch on a few. For a detailed list of all QML types and the documentation about those types, see http://bit.ly/17stfw3.

Creating Qt Quick applications in Qt Designer

In *Chapter 1*, *Getting Started with Qt Creator*, you gained basic familiarity with the Qt Designer for Qt Quick applications. Let's take another look before we recreate our calculator app in QML. The next screenshot shows the Qt Designer for the Qt Quick window:

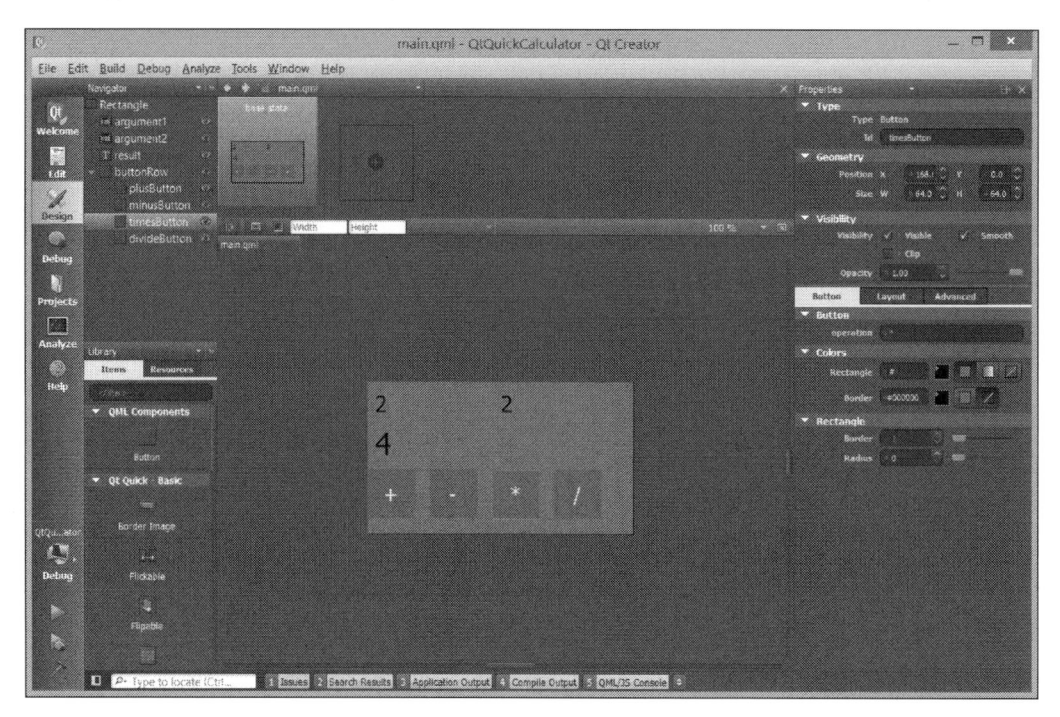

The Qt Designer for Qt Quick

Working from the left again, we have the following components:

- The view selector, showing that the Qt Designer view is active
- The object hierarchy for the file being edited, showing the parent-child relationship between visible items in that file
- Below the object hierarchy is a palette of the items you can drag out onto the QML editor pane
- Next to the object hierarchy is a summary of the states for the object
- Below the summary of states is the object editor for the QML file
- Finally, there's a property editor that lets you adjust the properties of the currently selected QML item

> Frankly, I find it easier to just write QML than to use the designer. The syntax takes a little getting used to, but what the designer is good for is previewing the QML you've written by hand and making minor adjustments to its layout.

Speaking of layout, before we see our sample code in detail, it's worth noting that QML has a rich dynamic layout system. Visible items have an `anchor` property, and you can anchor an item's sides against that of its neighbors or the parent view. You saw this briefly in *Chapter 1*, *Getting Started with Qt Creator*, where we made `MouseArea` as big as its parent. We'll also use that to control the layout of the calculator argument input lines and operator buttons.

Start making our sample code now by choosing **New File or Project...** from the **File** menu, and walk through the wizard to create a Qt Quick 2.0 application. Name your application `QtQuickCalculator`.

Creating a reusable button

Our calculator has a button for each operation. While we could make each button a separate rectangle and `MouseArea`, it's far easier to make a single QML button that encapsulates the behavior of a button, including the change in appearance when you press on it, the placement of the button label, and so forth.

Create a new QML file by right-clicking on the project and choosing **Add New...**, then from the Qt items, choose **QML File (Qt Quick 2)**. The button is a rectangle that contains a second rectangle, a `Text` label for the button, and a `MouseArea` region that handles button clicks. Name the file `Button.qml`, and edit it so that it reads as follows:

```
import QtQuick 2.0

Rectangle {
    id: button
    width: 64
    height: 64

    property alias operation: buttonText.text
    signal clicked

    color: "green"

    Rectangle {
        id: shade
        anchors.fill: button;
        color: "black"; opacity: 0
    }

    Text {
        id: buttonText
        anchors.centerIn: parent;
        color: "white"
        font.pointSize: 16
    }

    MouseArea {
        id: mouseArea
        anchors.fill: parent
        onClicked: {
            button.clicked();
        }
    }

    states: State {
        name: "pressed"; when: mouseArea.pressed == true
        PropertyChanges { target: shade; opacity: .4 }
    }
}
```

Working from the top of the file code:

- Within the scope of this file, the button's ID is simply `button`.
- It's 64 pixels in both width and height.
- The button has a single property configurable by its clients, the `operation` property. That property is actually an alias, meaning it's automatically setting the value of the `buttonText.text` property instead of being a separate field.
- The button emits a single signal, the `clicked` signal.
- The button's color is green.
- There's a rectangle that fills the button that is colored black, but has opacity of zero, meaning in normal use it's not visible, it's transparent. As the button is pressed, I adjust the opacity of this rectangle, to shade the button darker when it's being pressed.
- The `text` label of the button is `16` points in size, colored white, and centered in the button itself.
- The `MouseArea` region that accepts clicks for the button is the same size as the button and emits the clicked signal.
- The button has two states: the default state, and a second state pressed that occurs when the `mouseArea.pressed` property is `true` (because you are pressing the mouse button in the mouse area). When the state is pressed, I request a single `PropertyChange` event, changing the rectangle's opacity a bit to give a shadow over the button, darkening it.

You can actually see the two states of the button if you enter the Qt Designer (see the following screenshot). A state is just a name, a `when` clause indicating when the state is active, and a collection of `PropertyChanges` indicating what properties should change when the state is active. All visible QML items have a `state` property, which is just the name of the currently active state.

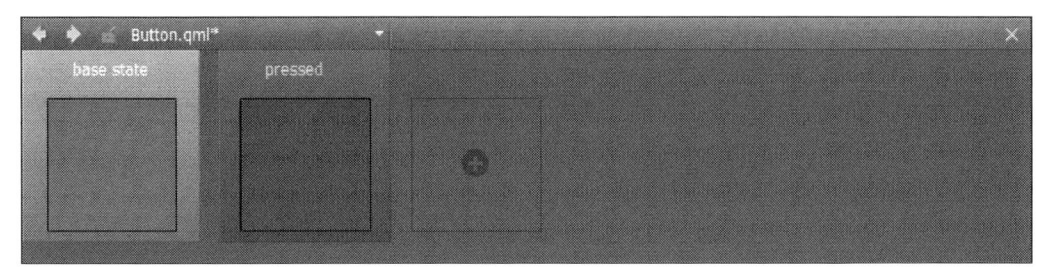

The states of the button

Note that QML uses signals and slots similar to Qt in C++, but there's no `emit` keyword. Instead, you declare the signal directly using the `signal` keyword and the name of the signal, and then you invoke the signal as if it were a function call. For each QML item's signal, the slot is named `on` followed by the signal name; for example, `onClicked`, `onPressed`, and so on. Thus, when we use the button, we write an `onClicked` handler for the `clicked` signal.

The calculator's main view

Go back to the editor and edit `main.qml` directly. We're going to declare our input lines, result line, and four operation buttons directly in code; you can do much of the same with the designer if you'd prefer, and then edit the code to match the following:

```
import QtQuick 2.0

Rectangle {
    width: 360
    height: 200
    color: "grey"

    TextInput {
        id: argument1
        anchors.left: parent.left
        width: 160
        anchors.top: parent.top
        anchors.topMargin: 10
        anchors.leftMargin: 10
        anchors.rightMargin: 10
        text: "2"
        font.pointSize: 18
    }

    TextInput {
        id: argument2
        anchors.right: parent.right
        width: 160
        anchors.top: parent.top
        anchors.topMargin: 10
        anchors.leftMargin: 10
        anchors.rightMargin: 10
        text: "2"
        font.pointSize: 18
    }
```

```
        Text {
            id: result
            anchors.left: parent.left
            anchors.right: parent.right
            anchors.top: argument2.bottom
            anchors.topMargin: 10
            anchors.leftMargin: 10
            anchors.rightMargin: 10
            text: "4"
            font.pointSize: 24
        }
        Row {
            id: buttonRow
            anchors.bottom: parent.bottom
            anchors.horizontalCenter: parent
            anchors.bottomMargin: 20
            spacing: 20
            Button {
                id: plusButton
                operation: "+"
                onClicked: result.text =
                   parseFloat(argument1.text) + parseFloat(argument2.text)
            }
            Button {
                id: minusButton
                operation: "-"
                onClicked: result.text =
                   parseFloat(argument1.text) - parseFloat(argument2.text)
            }
            Button {
                id: timesButton
                operation: "*"
                onClicked: result.text =
                   parseFloat(argument1.text) * parseFloat(argument2.text)
            }
            Button {
                id: divideButton
                operation: "/"
                onClicked: result.text =
                   parseFloat(argument1.text) / parseFloat(argument2.text)
            }
        }
    }
}
```

The view has two `TextInput` lines, a read-only `text` result line, and then the `operation` buttons, wrapped in a `Row` item to give them a horizontal layout. The base view for the calculator is `grey`, and is in a window 360 × 200 pixels. The controls are positioned as follows:

- The first input line is anchored to the top left of the parent window, with margins of 10 pixels. It's 160 pixels long and the default height for an 18-point `TextInput` field.
- The second input line is anchored to the right side of the parent, with a margin of 10 pixels at the top and right. It's also 160 pixels long, and the default height of an 18-point `TextInput` field.
- The result input line's top is anchored to the bottom of the input line, and to the left of the parent rectangle. It also has 10 pixels of margins on each side.
- The buttons are spaced 20 pixels apart in a `Row` item that's anchored to the bottom of the parent.

These anchors let the view reflow nicely if you resize the application window; the input lines spread across the width of the window, and the button bar on the bottom moves down as the window enlarges.

Each of the buttons has a `click` slot that obtains the floating-point interpretation of each of the input lines and performs the appropriate arithmetic operation. They're each instances of `Button`, the QML class I showed you in the previous section. Note the use of the JavaScript function `parseFloat` in the `onClicked` handlers: as you'd expect from what I mentioned before, there's support for the functions in the JavaScript runtime in QML, so we can just invoke JavaScript functions directly.

The following screenshot shows the completed calculator application. Note, when running the app, if you mouse over a button and press down, you'll see the shading darken (this isn't shown in the screenshot). This reflects the two states in the button that I showed you in the previous section:

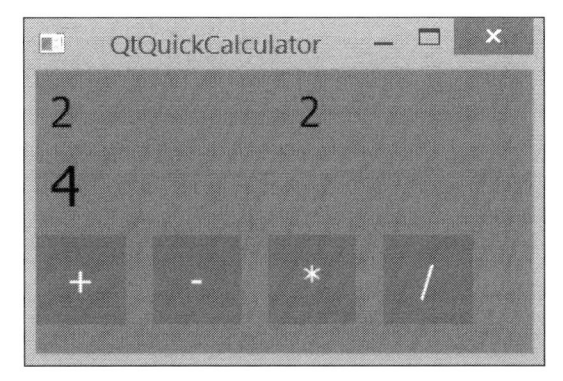

The completed Qt Quick calculator application

Learning more about Qt Quick and QML

Qt Quick was designed to create fluid applications that don't have a lot of deep widget complexity. Media hubs, photo viewers, phone dialers, web browsers, and other sorts of applications that don't need to match the look and feel of the host platform (or are on embedded systems where the host platform is all written in Qt Quick) are good examples of applications suiting the Qt Quick paradigm. For more information about Qt Quick with a plethora of examples that show you the breadth and power of the platform, see `http://bit.ly/16ULQ4V`.

Summary

Qt comes with not one, but two complementary GUI toolkits: Qt GUI, which takes a traditional widget-based approach to GUI development, and Qt Quick, which provides a declarative approach better-suited for platform-agnostic user interfaces for media boxes, some cell phone applications, automobile dashboards, and other embedded environments. For both, Qt offers Qt Designer, a drag-and-drop environment that lets you construct, configure, and preview your user interface as you build your application.

Core to Qt is the notion of signals and slots, Qt's answer to callbacks and events for handling the late-binding required of today's GUI applications. Qt objects can emit signals, which are type-safe function declarations, and other objects can connect to those signals, triggering method calls when the signals are emitted.

In the next chapter, you'll take a break from learning about Qt Creator and graphical user interface development to focus on one key aspect of application development: localization. I'll show you how to use Qt Linguist and Qt's localization functions to localize your application.

4
Localizing Your Application with Qt Linguist

Localization is an important, yet commonly neglected part of software development today. Most authors of applications, whether those applications are commercial or open source, have hopes to capture a large number of users for their application. Increasingly, this means supporting multiple languages in multiple locales; often needing support for multiple languages in one locale (think of French and English co-existing in Canada).

Qt has long had a framework for making applications easy to localize. With tools that help you avoid hardcoding strings in your application and a GUI named Qt Linguist to help manage translation, Qt eases the burden of localization throughout your application development cycle. In this chapter, we will look at Qt's strategy for localization, discussing the three tools (**lupdate**, **lrelease**, and **Qt Linguist**) Qt provides and how to use them, along with what you need to do as you write your application to take advantage of Qt's localization framework.

Understanding the task of localization

Localizing your application has several phases, which typically overlap throughout a project. These phases are:

1. As you write your application, you place strings to localize your application in a specific way so that Qt can identify the strings as needing localization.
2. Periodically, you extract all the strings in your application and give them to translators to translate.
3. Translators provide translations for the strings in your application.
4. You compile translation files with the translated strings for each language you want to support.

Qt provides four tools to facilitate these phases:

- The `tr` and `qsTr` functions for C++ and QML let you identify the strings in your application that require localization
- The `lupdate` command generates a list of the strings that need localization in your application
- Translators use Qt Linguist to provide translations of the strings in your application
- The `lrelease` command takes the translated strings from Qt Creator and packages them in a format for your application to consume

The following figure shows how these phases interact:

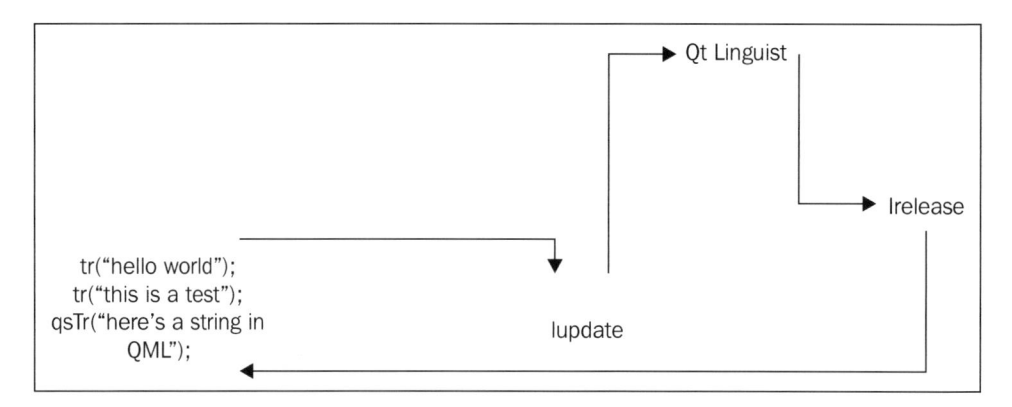

The lupdate/Linguist/lrelease cycle

Software development is iterative, and localization is no exception. Small projects may prefer to do the localization just once, or perhaps twice, waiting until the application is nearly done before submitting the application strings for localization. Larger applications, or larger companies with a dedicated staff of translators, may prefer a more iterative approach, going through the localization cycle several times throughout application development. Qt supports both the models.

Marking strings for localization

All the way back in *Chapter 1, Getting Started with Qt Creator*, I told you to always mark your strings for localization using the `tr` and `qsTr` functions: `tr` for C++ and `qsTr` for QML strings. Doing so has two key advantages for you. First, it enables Qt to find every string that needs localization. Second, if you install a Qt translator object in your application and provide a translation file, the strings you wrap with these functions are automatically replaced by their localized equivalent.

Let's examine the use of `tr` in more detail. All Qt objects that include the `Q_OBJECT` macro in their declaration include the `tr` function. You've seen it with one argument, as shown in the following line of code:

```
button = new QPushButton(tr("&Quit"), this);
```

The leading `&` in the string isn't for the `tr` function, but for the keyboard accelerators; you can prefix a letter with `&` and it gets the default system (*Alt* for Windows, *command* for Apple, and *Control* for Linux). The `tr` function uses the string you pass as the string in the user interface if no translated version of the string appears in the application's current translation table, or uses the string in the current translation table if one exists.

The `tr` function can take a second argument, a disambiguation context that `tr` uses for the same string that may require different translations. It can also handle strings with plurals, as shown in the following line of code:

```
tr("%n item(s) replaced", "", count);
```

Depending on the value of count and the locale, a different string is returned. So, a native English translation might return "0 items replaced", "1 item replaced", "2 items replaced", and so on, while a French translation could return "0 item remplacé", "1 item remplacé", "2 items remplacés", and so on.

The `qsTr` function in QML works similarly, but it does not have the flexibility that the `tr` method has for disambiguation or handling plurals.

Localizing your application with Qt Linguist

Once you've marked your strings using `tr` or `qsTr`, you need to generate a table of those strings for Qt Linguist to localize. You can do this using the `lupdate` command, which takes your `.pro` file and walks your sources looking for strings to localize, and creates an XML file for Qt Linguist of the strings you need to translate. You'll do this once for each language you want to support. When doing this, it's best to name the resulting files systematically; one way to do that is to use the name of the project file, followed by a dash, followed by the ISO-639-2 language code for the language.

A concrete example is in order. This chapter has `QtLinguistExample`; I can run `lupdate` using a command like this to create a list of strings that I'll translate to Esperanto (ISO-639-2 language code EPO):

```
% lupdate -pro .\QtLinguistExample.pro -ts .\QtLinguistExample-epo.ts
```

Where the `-pro` file indicates the `.pro` file that contains the list of sources to scan for strings to translate, and the `-ts` argument indicates the name of the translation files to be written.

> You'll need `lupdate` in your path, of course. How you set your path will depend on whether you're working on Windows, Mac OS X, or Linux, and where you've installed Qt. Some installations of Qt may update your path automatically, while others may not. On my Windows machine, for example, I find `lupdate` at `C:\qt\5.1.0\msvc2012_64\bin\lupdate.exe`.

The `.ts` file is an XML file with tags to indicate the strings to translate their context in your application's source code, and so forth. Qt Linguist will save the translations to the QM file as well, but don't worry, `lupdate` is smart enough not to overwrite existing translations if you run it again after providing some translations.

Qt Linguist is a GUI application; when you start it you'll see a screen very similar to the next screenshot:

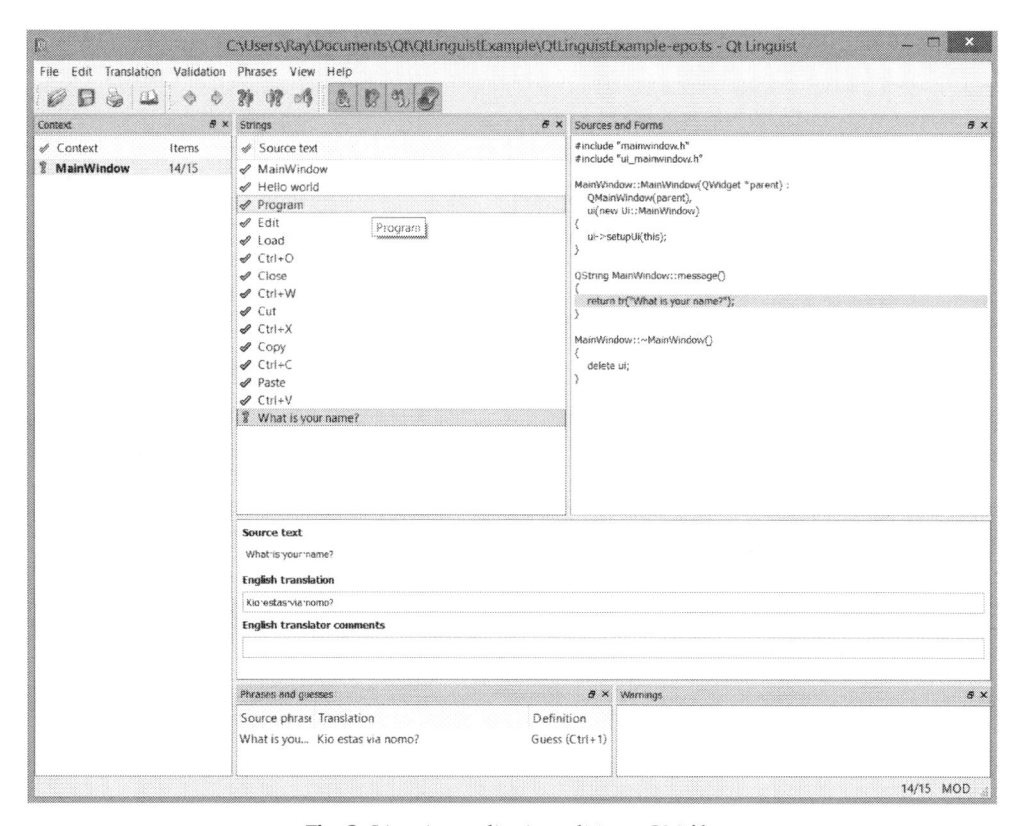

The Qt Linguist application editing a QM file

To begin, you need to open a .ts file you generated by navigating to **File | Open**, and choosing a translation file. You'll be prompted for the destination language, and then you're given a list of the strings it found. You—or your translators—need only to walk through each string and enter the corresponding string in the translated language. As you do so, you can see the context of the string in the source code in the right-most pane; the line of source from which the string was captured is highlighted.

Qt Linguist lets you track which strings you've translated and which still need translation. The icon to the left of each of the strings can be:

- A black question mark indicating that a string has yet to be translated
- A yellow question mark indicating that the string doesn't pass all of Qt Linguist's validation tests, but you're ignoring the failures
- An exclamation point indicating that the string you've provided doesn't pass Qt Linguist's validation tests
- A yellow checkbox indicating that you've provided a translation, but Qt Creator may have found a problem with it
- A green checkbox indicating that the string has been translated and is ready to go

Qt Linguist provides some simple validation tests, such as ensuring that strings with arguments such as printf have the same number of arguments in each translation.

Qt Linguist also supports phrase books; you may be able to download a phrase book with common strings already localized to the language you're targeting.

At any point, you can generate a translation file for inclusion in your application by running lrelease. For example, to create one for my Esperanto strings, I'd use lrelease as follows:

```
% lrelease .\QtLinguistExample-epo.ts .\QtLinguistExample-epo.qm
```

This takes the incoming .ts file, and generates a .qm file with the strings. The .qm files are highly compressed binary files used by Qt directly in the process of rendering your application.

Including localized strings in your application

In order to supply translated strings to the `tr` and `qsTr` functions in your application, your application needs to include a `QTranslator` object to read the `.ts` files and replace the strings provided to `tr` and `qsTr` with their translated counterparts. We do this in your main entry point function, as shown in the following block of code:

```
QApplication a(argc, argv);
QTranslator translator;
bool result = translator.load("QtLinguistExample-epo.qm");
a.installTranslator(&translator);

    // Other window setup stuff goes here

return a.exec();
```

This code allocates a `QTranslator` object, and loads the indicated translation file into the translator before installing it into `QApplication`. In this example, we're hardcoding the language to localize to Esperanto.

Note that if you want to support the locale as picked by the system, we might choose to do it this way:

```
QString locale = QLocale::system().name();
QTranslator translator;
translator.load(QString("QtLinguistExample-") + locale);
```

This determines the system locale, and attempts to load the localized string file for the system's current locale.

For this to work, the `.qm` files for the application need to be locatable by the application. They should be in the output directory; one way to do this during development is to turn off shadow builds in Qt Creator, under **Build Settings** in the **Projects** pane. As you build your application's installer—a platform-specific task outside the scope of this book—you need to include your `.qm` files with the application binary.

Localizing special things – currencies and dates with QLocale

A common thing you may need to do is localize currencies and dates. Qt makes this easy, although the solution isn't obvious until you've thought about it a bit.

First, you should know about the `arg` method of `QString`. It replaces an escaped number with the formatted version of its argument; if we write:

```
QString s = new QString("%1 %2").arg("a").arg("b");
```

Then `s` contains the string `a b`. Second, you should know about the `toString` method of `QLocale`, which formats its argument in a locale-specific way.

So, we could write:

```
QString currencyValue = QString("%1 %2")
    .arg(tr("$")).arg(QLocale::toString(value, 'g', 2)
```

This uses `tr` to localize the currency symbol, and the `QLocale` class's static method `toString` to convert the value to a string with the locale-specific decimal separator (period in the U.S. and Canada, comma in Europe).

Date formatting is similar: the `toString` method of `QLocale` has overloads for the `QDateTime`, `QDate`, and `QTime` arguments, so you can simply write:

```
QDateTime whenDateTime = QDateTime::currentDateTime();
QString when = QLocale::toString(whenDate);
```

This gets the current date and time and stores it in `whenDateTime`, and then makes a string out of it using the locale's default formatting. The `toString` method can take a second argument that determines the output format. It can be one of the following:

- `QLocale::LongFormat`, which uses the long version of month and day names
- `QLocale::ShortFormat`, which uses the short version of day and month names
- `QLocale::NarrowFormat`, which provides the narrowest form of formatting for the date and time

Summary

Localizing applications with Qt is easy using Qt Linguist and the localization framework in Qt. To use the framework, though, you must mark your strings to localize with `tr` or `qsTr` in your source code wherever they appear. Once you do so, you can create a source file of strings to translate with Qt Linguist using Qt's `lupdate` command, and then provide translations for each string. Once you've provided the translations, you compile them using `lrelease`, and then include them in your application by installing a `QTranslator` object in your application's `main` function and loading the translation table generated by `lrelease`.

In the next chapter, we will look at another important aspect of software development Qt Creator supports, which is performance analysis with the QML Profiler and Valgrind.

5
Performance Optimization with Qt Creator

We don't use performance analysis tools every day, but we're glad they're there when we need them. Commercial tools like the ones that come with Microsoft Visual Studio or standalone tools such as IBM's Rational Rose Purify can set you back a pretty pile of change—fortunately, Qt Creator has most of what you need built-in, or has support for working with open source tools to help you profile the runtime and memory performance of your application.

In this chapter, we will see how we can perform runtime profiling of QML applications using the QML performance analyzer, and learn how to read the report it generates. We then turn our attention to memory performance analysis with Valgrind using Qt Creator, which is a free option to look for memory leaks and heap corruption on the Linux platform.

The QML performance analyzer

Qt Quick applications are supposed to be fast, with smooth, fluid user interfaces. In many cases, that's easy to accomplish with QML; the contributors to QML and the Qt Quick runtime have put a great deal of effort into creating an environment that performs well under a wide variety of circumstances. Sometimes, however, try as you might, you may find that you just can't squeeze the performance that you'd like out of your application. Some mistakes are obvious, such as:

- Doing a lot of compute-intensive tasks between state changes or actions that trigger drawing operations

- Excessively complex view hierarchies with thousands of elements on the display at once
- Running on very limited hardware (often in combination with the first two problems)

Knuth famously said that "Premature optimization is the root of all evil", and he's definitely right. However, there might come a time when you need to measure the performance of your application, and Qt Creator includes a special performance analyzer for just this purpose. With it, you can see how much time your application spends in each QML method, as well as measure critical aspects of your application that are at the edge of your control, like how long it takes to create your application's view hierarchy.

Let's take a closer look.

QtSlowButton – a Qt Quick application in need of performance tuning

Let's analyze the performance of `QtSlowButton`, a poorly-performing example program I put together for you in this chapter. `QtSlowButton` has two QML components: a button based on the calculator button from *Chapter 3, Designing Your Application with Qt Designer*, and a view with buttons you can press. Here's the implementation of the button:

```
import QtQuick 2.0
Rectangle {
    id: button
    width: 128
    height: 64
    property alias label: buttonText.text
    property int delay: 0
    color: "green"
    Rectangle {
        id: shade
        anchors.fill: button;
        color: "black"; opacity: 0
    }
```

```
    Text {
        id: buttonText
        anchors.centerIn: parent;
        color: "white"
        font.pointSize: 16
    }
    MouseArea {
        id: mouseArea
        anchors.fill: parent
        onClicked: {
            for(var i = 0; i < button.delay; i++);
        }
    }
    states: [
        State {
            name: "pressed"; when: mouseArea.pressed == true
            PropertyChanges { target: shade; opacity: .4 }
        }
    ]
}
```

Each button simply runs a `for` loop when you push it; its `delay` property controls how many times it cycles through the loop. In addition, each button has a label, which the button draws in the center of the clickable area.

The main user interface consists of three buttons in a `Column region`, labeled `fast`, `medium`, and `slow`, with progressively longer delays:

```
import QtQuick 2.0
Rectangle {
    width: 180
    height: 360
    Column
    {
        spacing: 20
        Button
        {
            delay: 10000;
            label: "fast";
        }
```

```
        Button
        {
            delay: 100000;
            label: "medium";
        }
        Button
        {
            delay: 300000;
            label: "slow";
        }
    }
}
```

You can either load the source project that comes with this book for this example, or you can create a new Qt Quick project and make a button and main view with this code.

To analyze the application's performance:

1. Build the application.
2. Choose **QML Profiler** from the **Analyze** menu. The application will start, and Qt Creator will switch to the **Analyze** view.
3. In the application itself, click on each application button a few times. You will be expected to wait after you click on each button.
4. Quit the application.

> The QML Profiler uses TCP/IP to make a connection between the running application and the profiler, by default on port 3768. You may need to tinker with your host's firewall settings to get things to work correctly. On Windows, be sure to permit the connection in the **Windows Firewall** dialog that appears.

The following screenshot shows the **Analyze** view after running your application. The QML Profiler has three tabs, and shows the first by default:

- The first tab is the timeline, indicating what things happened at what point through the application, and how long they took
- The second tab lists the events the QML application processed, and how much time was spent in each event
- The third tab lists the JavaScript functions the program encountered while running, and how long the application spent in total to run each function

In the following screenshot, I've clicked on the **Handling Signal** row to expand the signals the application handled. You can see it handled one signal, `onClicked`, a total of three times, and the amount of time spent in each is shown as varying bars on the graph. Clearly, if the application were doing something that could be optimized, there'd be an opportunity for performance improvement here:

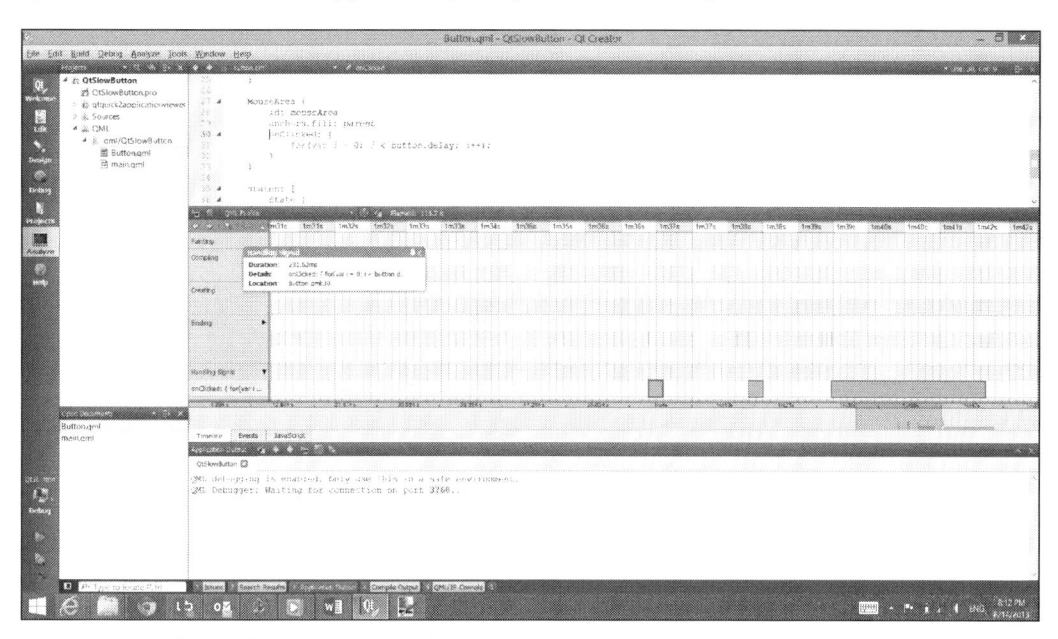

The Timeline view, showing how much time was spent in my onClicked method

The next screenshot shows a different view of this information, indicating that up to the limit of numerical accuracy, the application spent all of its measured time in the `onClicked` handler for the button: clearly a performance "hot spot" in this case. Interestingly, every incident of my JavaScript is measured here, including the $when clause that puts the opaque filter in front of the button when it's pressed. Looking at the **JavaScript** view can be very helpful if you need to look at where things are happening in your application in a broad sense:

The total time spent running different bits of JavaScript in QtSlowButton

The next screenshot is likely the most interesting for performance geeks, because it shows the amount of time QML spent for each and every event it handled running the application. Again, we see the `onClicked` handler consuming the lion's share of the processor resources, but other things like the creation of the rectangles for the view and the variable binding for the state of a push button are shown as well. Typically, we'll use the **JavaScript** view to get the broad picture of where the problems in your application are, while you'll use the **Events** view to zero in on specific problems:

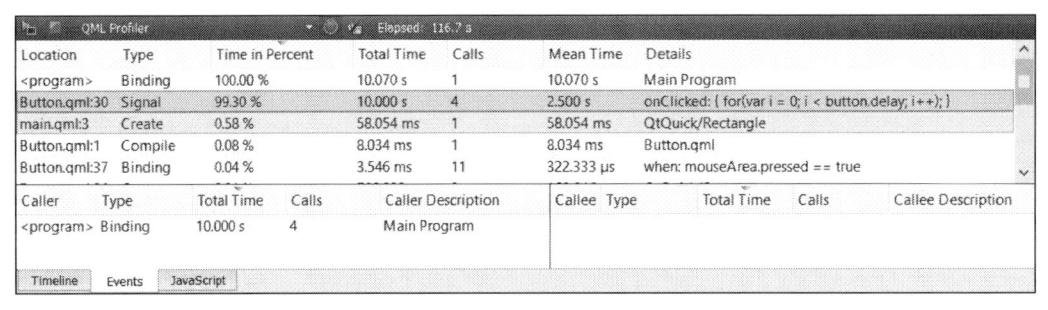

The Events view of the QML Profiler, showing each and every event in QtSlowButton

Finding memory leaks with Valgrind

As we discussed in *Chapter 3, Designing Your Application with Qt Designer*, you should really get in the habit of using Qt's parent-child relationship when managing memory for classes of `QObject` in your application to avoid memory leaks. In my time writing Qt applications, the only time I've had to deal with memory leaks was when I didn't do that. In addition, using classes such as `QSharedPointer` for pointers that aren't based on `QObject` is a good idea too.

Sometimes, though, you may introduce a memory leak you can't find on your own. In that case, a tool such as Valgrind can be a lifesaver; it tracks every memory allocation and free operation in your application, alerting you when your program terminates if it hasn't freed all the memory it allocates.

Unfortunately, Valgrind is a Linux-only tool. If you're writing pure Qt code, this shouldn't be a serious issue for you even if you're developing on Windows or Mac OS X, because you can port your application to Linux and run it in Valgrind there. To do that, you'll want to use an application such as VMware Fusion, VMware Player, Microsoft HyperV, or Parallels to set up a virtual machine running Linux (I like to use Ubuntu), install Qt Creator, and get your code running there. (Unfortunately, if you have Windows-specific code or libraries in your application, this isn't an option.)

> If you build your application for Windows, a commercial leak detector such as Rational Purify may be an option.

Before continuing, you should make sure you have Qt Creator running under a Linux distribution, and install Valgrind from `http://bit.ly/14QwiQZ` or use your package manager. For example, on Ubuntu, I can install Valgrind with the following command:

```
sudo apt-get install valgrind
```

When you use Valgrind, you actually run your application inside of Valgrind; instead of starting your application, you start Valgrind, which starts your application.

QtLeakyButton – a Qt C++ application in need of memory help

The `QtLeakyButton` application does one thing: it presents a button that when clicked, allocates 512 KB of RAM. The following is the code (you can either run the sample that accompanies this book, or create a Qt GUI application with a single button and a label and use this code for your `MainWindow` class):

```cpp
// mainwindow.h
#ifndef MAINWINDOW_H
#define MAINWINDOW_H

#include <QMainWindow>

namespace Ui {
    class MainWindow;
}

class MainWindow : public QMainWindow
{
    Q_OBJECT

public:
    explicit MainWindow(QWidget *parent = 0);
    ~MainWindow();
```

```
public slots:
    void leakPressed();

private:
    Ui::MainWindow *ui;
    int m_count;
};

#endif // MAINWINDOW_H

// mainwindow.cpp

#include "mainwindow.h"
#include "ui_mainwindow.h"

MainWindow::MainWindow(QWidget *parent) :
    QMainWindow(parent),
    ui(new Ui::MainWindow),
    m_count(0)
{
    ui->setupUi(this);
    connect(ui->leakButton, SIGNAL(clicked()),
            this, SLOT(leakPressed()));
}

MainWindow::~MainWindow()
{
    delete ui;
}

void MainWindow::leakPressed()
{
    void *p = new char[512 * 1024];
    m_count++;
    ui->leakCount->setText(QString::number(m_count));
}
```

The MainWindow class has an integer counter and a ui slot for the instantiated form. The MainWindow constructor instantiates this form, and then connects the clicked signal of leakButton to MainWnidow::leakPressed. The leakPressed method just allocates memory and bumps the counter, updating the counter with the number of times you've pressed the button.

To use Valgrind, we need to add a new run target to your application. To accomplish this, do the following:

1. Click on **Projects** on the left, and then on **Run**.
2. Click on **Add**.
3. For **Name**, enter `valgrind`.
4. For **Executable**, add the path to Valgrind (usually `/usr/bin/valgrind`).
5. For arguments, enter the following:

    `-q --tool=memcheck --leak-check=full --leak-resolution=low ./<your-app-target-name>`

6. For **Working Directory**, enter `$BUILDDIR`.

Now we can select the Valgrind run target for your application. We need to do this with the debug build because Valgrind needs the debug symbols in our application to produce a meaningful report. To use Valgrind, start the application and click on the button a few times. The Valgrind process outputs information continually, but most of the output comes after we quit the application.

Valgrind produces a lot of output, which can take some time to sort through. We're looking for the leak summary, which indicates the number of bytes definitely lost and indirectly lost. The blocks that are definitely lost are memory you've allocated and not freed; indirectly lost memory is memory leaked because it's referred to by another pointer, and the referring pointer wasn't freed. The output will look something like:

```
X bytes in 1 blocks are definitely lost in loss record n of m
   at 0x........: function_name (filename:line number)
```

Here, X indicates the number of bytes that were leaked, and the address of the leaked block is shown on the second line. The record numbers indicate internal record numbers used by the application's memory allocator, and probably won't help you very much.

We should really focus on leaks in our application, because it's possible that Qt may have leaks of its own. Valgrind supports suppression files, which indicate what leaks should be ignored; if you can find and download one for the versions of Qt you're building against, you can include a reference to the suppression file by modifying the argument line to read:

`-q --tool=memcheck --leak-check=full --leak-resolution=low --suppressions=suppresion.txt ./[your-app-target-name]`

Finding memory leaks in your application is part art and part science. It's a good exercise to go through periodically during application development, to ensure that leaks you may introduce are quickly found while you're most familiar with the new code you're running.

Summary

Qt Creator provides the QML analyzer, which lets you perform runtime analysis of your Qt applications. You can see a graph in time of how your application is running, as well as dive into detail about how your application spends its time drawing, binding to variables, and executing JavaScript.

Qt Creator also integrates well with Valgrind on Linux, letting you look for memory leaks in your application. Using Valgrind on Linux, you can see blocks that were allocated but not freed, and more importantly, how big they are and where in the code they were allocated, giving you a head start in determining why they were not freed.

In the next chapter, we turn from specific parts of Qt Creator to one of its most exciting aspects in general: the ability to use Qt Creator to compile and test applications for mobile platforms such as Google Android.

6
Developing Mobile Applications with Qt Creator

Qt and mobile development have a long history. Qt's beginnings included early releases on Linux Personal Digital Assistants in the late nineties and at the turn of this century. Since then, it's been ported to a number of mobile environments, including the mobile variants of Linux that Nokia shipped such as MeeGo, as well as Symbian. While Symbian and MeeGo have come and gone, Qt's acceptance of mobile platforms lives on, most recently with support for Android.

In this chapter, we talk a little about writing mobile applications, and then learn how to set up Qt Creator to write applications for Android. It's worth noting right at the outset that while we will leverage everything you have learned about Qt development developing a mobile application, we also need to understand how the environments that mobile software runs in are different from traditional desktop and laptop environments, and how to design for those constraints. Once we understand those differences, writing software for Android with Qt is a snap!

A mobile software development primer

The key difference to remember when developing software for any mobile platform — such as a cell phone or tablet — is that every resource is at a premium. The device is smaller, meaning that:

- Your user will pay less attention to your application, and use it for shorter periods of time
- The screen is smaller, so you can display less information on the display (don't be fooled by the high-dot pitch of today's displays: reading 6-point font on a 4-inch display is no fun, high pixel densities or not)
- The processor and graphics processing unit are slower

- There's less RAM and less graphics memory
- There's less persistent storage for your application's data
- The network is slower, by as much as three orders of magnitude

Let's look at each of these in more detail.

User attention is at a premium

Can you walk and chew gum at the same time? I can't—but many people walk, chew gum, and use their mobile device all at the same time. (Worse, some even drive while using their devices!) It's very rare for an application on a cell phone or tablet to have 100 percent of the user's attention for more than a few minutes at a time. A good rule of thumb is that the smaller the device, the more likely the user is to treat it as something to pick up and glance at, or use it while they're doing something else.

The limited attention your user pays to your application has three key consequences:

- Your application must be fast. Mobile devices are no place for extra progress bars, spinning cursors, or lengthy splash screens.
- Your application must be succinct. The best mobile applications show data on only a page or two, having very flat navigation hierarchies. A common structure is to have a single screen of information, and a single screen with preferences that lets you configure what information should be shown (such as what location for which you're getting the information). Favor clear iconography over verbose text—if you can't draw, find someone who can, or buy icons from a site such as *The Noun Project* (http://bit.ly/1fvBsnu).
- Your application must be accessible. Buttons should be big (a good guideline is that no hit target in your application should be smaller than the pad of your finger, about a square centimeter), and the text should be bigger, if possible.

For these reasons, Qt Quick is the better choice for most mobile applications you'll write. You can create smooth and responsive applications that are visually pleasing and don't overwhelm your users.

Computational resources are at a premium

Mobile devices must carry their power source with them: that means batteries. While batteries have improved over the last twenty years, they haven't kept up with Moore's Law; most of the improvements have been on the processor side, as processors have become smaller and dissipate less heat in the course of a normal operation.

Nonetheless, mobile devices aren't as fast as desktops or laptops—a good way to think about it is that the last generation's processor design probably scales well for mobile devices today. That's not to say that mobile devices are slow, just that they're slower. Equally important, you can't run the processor or graphics processor at full tilt without seriously affecting battery life.

Qt—especially Qt Quick—is optimized for low power consumption, but there are still things you can do to help squeeze the best performance out of your mobile application:

- **Don't poll**: This is probably the single most important point. Use Qt's asynchronous signal-slot mechanism wherever possible, and consider multithreading using `QThread`, Qt's multithreading environment, if you need to do something in the background. The more your application sleeps, the further it prolongs the battery life.

- **Avoid gratuitous animations**: Some animation is both customary and important in today's applications; well-thought-out animations can help to orient the user as to where they've come from in an application's user interface and where they're going. But don't flash, blink, or otherwise animate just to see pixels move; under the hood a lot has to happen to move those pixels, and that can eat battery life.

- **Use the network judiciously**: Most mobile devices have at least two radios (cellular and Wi-Fi); some have more. Accessing the network should be seen as a necessary evil, because the radios consume power when transmitting and receiving data. And don't forget data parsing, either: if you're parsing a lot of data, you're likely running the CPU at full tilt to do the heavy lifting, and that means lower battery life.

Network resources are at a premium

I've already warned you about the high cost to the battery for using the network. To add insult to injury, most mobile devices run on networks that can be up to three orders of magnitude slower than a desktop: your office desktop may have gigabit Ethernet, but in many parts of the world, a megabit per second is considered fast. This situation is rapidly improving, as network operators deploy cellular wireless networks such as **Long Term Evolution** (**LTE**) and Wi-Fi hotspots everywhere, but it's by no means uniformly available. On a recent trip in California, in the course of eight hours, my cellular network connectivity throughput ran the gamut from faster than my cable modem (running at 25 megabits per second) down to the dreaded megabit-a-second that can make a large web page crawl.

For most applications, you should be fine using the **Hypertext Transfer Protocol** (**HTTP**); Qt's `QNetworkAccessManager` class implements HTTP and HTTPS, and using HTTP means that you can build web services to support your backend in a standard way.

If you're developing a game or a very custom kind of application, you may need to build a custom protocol. Consider using `QTcpSocket` or `QUdpSocket` for your network protocol, remembering of course that TCP is a reliable protocol, while with UDP there's no guarantee of your data reaching its destination; reliability is up to you.

Storage resources are at a premium

Mobile devices typically use all solid-state memory. Although solid-state memory has come down in price significantly in the last several years, it's still not as cheap as the rotating magnetic memory that makes up the disk drives in most desktops and many laptops. As a result, mobile devices may have as little as 8 GB of flash memory for persistent storage, or if you're lucky, 16 or 32 GB. That's shared across the system and all applications; your application shouldn't use more than a few gigabytes at most, and that's only if your user is expecting it—say, for a podcast application. That should be the sum total of the size of your application, its static resources such as audio and video, and anything it might download and cache from the network.

Equally important, the runtime size of your application needs to be smaller. Most mobile devices have between a half GB and 2 GB of dynamic RAM available; the system shares this across all running applications, so it's important to allocate what you need and free it when you're done. Qt's memory management system, which I explained in *Chapter 3*, *Designing Your Application with Qt Designer,* and *Chapter 5*, *Performance Optimization with Qt Creator*, comes in handy here.

Finally, don't forget that your graphics textures can eat valuable GPU memory as well. While Qt manages the GPU for you, whether you're using Qt or Qt Quick, you can write an application that consumes all of a device's texture memory, making it difficult, or impossible, for the native OS to render what it needs if it needs to interrupt your application.

To port or not to port?

To paraphrase the immortal bard, that's the question. With Qt's incredible flexibility across numerous platforms, the temptation to grab an existing application and port it can be overwhelming; especially in the vertical markets where you have a piece of custom software written in Qt for the desktop and a customer who wants "the same thing" for the latest mobile device for their mobile workers. In general, the best advice I can offer is to avoid porting UI, and only port the business logic in an application if it seems well-behaved for mobile devices.

UI ported from the desktop or a laptop environment seldom works well on mobile devices. The user's operating patterns are just too different: what a person wants to do while seated at a desktop or laptop is just not the same as what they want or can do standing up, walking around, or in brief spurts in a conference room, cafeteria, or café. If you're porting from one mobile device to another, it may not be so bad; for example, a developer with a Qt application for MeeGo, Nokia's Linux-based platform, shouldn't have too much of a problem bringing their application to Qt on Android.

Porting business logic may be a safer bet, assuming it doesn't make heavy use of the CPU, network, or dynamic or static storage. Qt offers a wrapper for SQLite through QtSQL, and many enterprise applications use that for local storage. That's a reasonable alternative for data storage, and most HTTP-based networking applications shouldn't be too hard on the network layer, as long as they have reasonable caching policies and don't make too many requests for data too often. But if the application uses a lot of storage or has a persistent network connection, it's time to rearchitect and rewrite.

A word on testing

Testing any application is important, but mobile applications require additional effort in testing, especially Android applications. There's a wide variety of devices on the market, and users expect your application to perform well on any device they may have.

The most important thing you can do is test your application on real devices, as many of them as you can get your hands on, if you're interested in releasing your application commercially. While as you will see, the Android SDK used by Qt Creator comes with an emulator that can run your Android application on your desktop or laptop, running in an emulator is no substitute for running on the device. A lot of things are different, from the size of the hardware itself to having a touch screen, and of course the network connection and raw processing power.

Fortunately, Android devices aren't terribly expensive, and there are an awful lot of them around. If you're just starting out, eBay or the Google Play Store can be a good place to shop for an inexpensive used or new device. If you're a student or budding entrepreneur, don't forget that many family members may have an Android device you can borrow, or you can use the Android cell phone that you already have.

What and when should you test? Everything and often! On a multiweek project, you should never be more than a few days away from a build running on a device. The longer you spend writing code that you haven't tested on a device, the more assumptions you may be making about how the device will perform.

Be sure not to just test your application in good circumstances, but in bad ones as well. Network connectivity is a prime example; you should test your error handling in cases with no network coverage. If you have good network coverage where you're working, one trick you can use is to put the device in a metal cookie tin or paint can; the metal attenuates the signal and has the same effect as the signal being lost in the real world (say, in a tunnel or on the subway).

Setting up Qt Creator for Android

Android's functionality is delimited in API levels; Qt for Android supports Android level 10 and above: that's Android 2.3.3, a variant of Gingerbread. Fortunately, most devices in the field today are at least Gingerbread, making Qt for Android a viable development platform for millions of devices.

Downloading all the pieces

To get started with Qt Creator for Android, you're going to need to download a lot of stuff. Let's get started:

- Begin with a release of Qt for Android, which was either part of the Qt installation you downloaded in *Chapter 1, Getting Started with Qt Creator,* or you need to go back and download it from `http://bit.ly/13G4Jfr`
- The Android developer tools require a current version of the **Java Development Kit** (**JDK**) (not just the runtime, the Java Runtime Environment, but the whole kit and caboodle); download it from `http://bit.ly/14HAaj4`, or you may be able to get things to work with Linux using OpenJDK at `http://bit.ly/1deNuTX`
- You need the latest Android **Software Development Kit** (**SDK**), which you can download for Mac OS X, Linux, or Windows from `http://bit.ly/146nsPl`
- You need the latest Android **Native Development Kit** (**NDK**), which you can download from `http://bit.ly/16UYK5o`
- You need the current version of Ant, the Java build tool, which you can download from `http://bit.ly/18AVI1F`

Download, unzip, and install each of these, in this order. On Windows, I installed the Android SDK and NDK by unzipping them to the root of my hard drive, and installed the JDK in the default location I was offered.

Setting up the environment variables

Once you install the JDK, you need to be sure that you've set your `JAVA_HOME` environment variable to point to the directory where it was installed. How you do this differs from platform to platform; on a Mac OS X or Linux box, you'd edit your `.bashrc`, `.tcshrc`, or the others; on Windows you'll go into system properties, click on **Environment Variables...**, and add the `JAVA_HOME` variable. The path should be to the base of the JDK directory: for me, it was `C:\Program Files\Java\jdk1.7.0_25\`, although the path for you will depend on where you installed the JDK and what version you installed. (Make sure you set the path with the trailing directory separator; the Android SDK is pretty fussy about that sort of thing.)

Next up, you need to update your `PATH` variable to point to all the stuff you just installed. Again, it's an environment variable, and you'll need to add the following:

- The `bin` directory of your JDK
- The `android\sdk\tools` directory
- The `android\sdk\platform-tools` directory

For me, on my Windows 8 computer, my `PATH` variable includes the following now:

```
...C:\Program Files\Java\jdk1.7.0_25\bin;C:\adt-bundle-
windows-x86_64-20130729\sdk\tools;;C:\adt-bundle-
windows-x86_64-20130729\sdk\platform-tools;...
```

Don't forget the separators: on Windows, it's a semicolon (`;`) on Mac OS X and Linux it's a colon (`:`).

At this point, it's a good idea to restart your computer (if you're running Windows) or log out and log back in to make sure all these settings take effect. If you're on a Mac OS X or Linux box, you may be able to start a new terminal and have the same effect (or reload your shell configuration file) instead, but I like the idea of restarting at this point to ensure that the next time I start everything up, it'll work correctly.

Finishing the Android SDK installation

Now we need to use the Android SDK tools to ensure you have a full version of the SDK for at least one Android API level installed. We'll need to start Eclipse, the Android SDK's development environment, and run the Android SDK manager. To do this, follow the ensuing steps:

1. Find Eclipse. It's probably in the Eclipse directory of the directory you installed the Android SDK in. If Eclipse doesn't start, check your `JAVA_HOME` and `PATH` variables; odds are Eclipse can't find the Java environment it needs to run.

2. Click on **OK** when Eclipse prompts you for a workspace. This doesn't matter; you won't use Eclipse except to download Android SDK components.

3. Click on the Android SDK Manager button in the Eclipse toolbar (circled in the next screenshot):

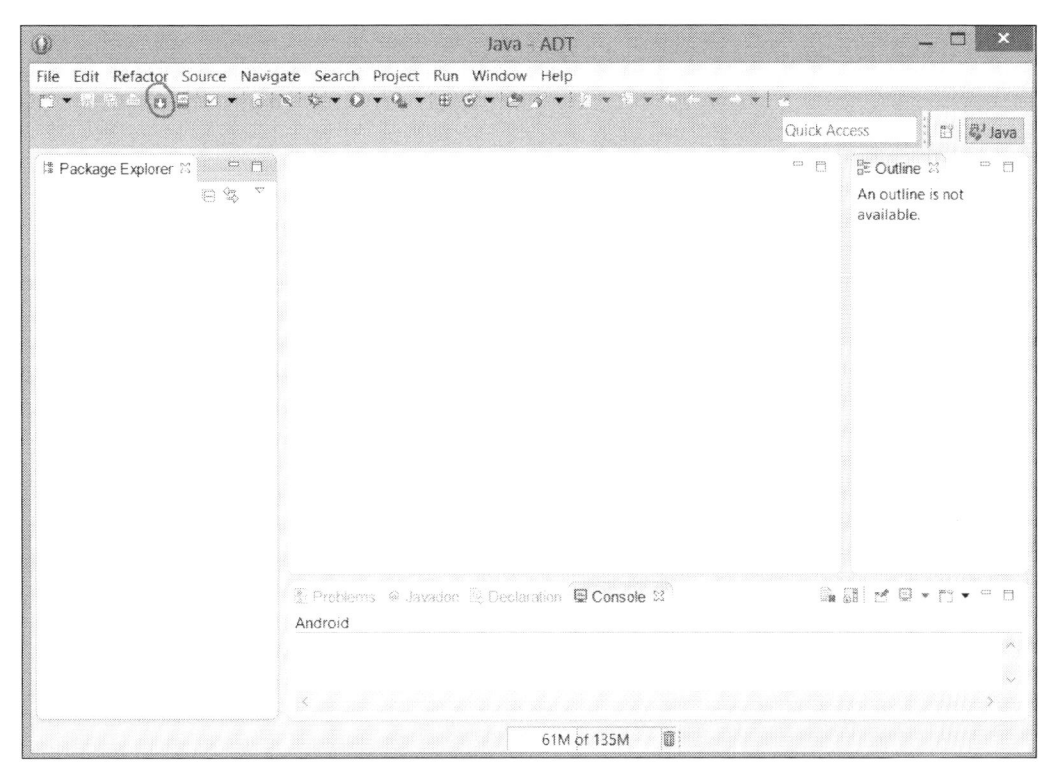

The Eclipse SDK, with the Android SDK Manager button circled

4. Make sure you have at least one Android API level above API Level 10 installed, along with the Google USB Driver (you'll need that to debug on hardware).

5. Quit Eclipse.

Next, let's see if the Android Debug Bridge—the software component that transfers your executables to your Android device and supports on-device debugging—is working as it should. Fire up a shell prompt and type `adb`. If you see a lot of output and no error, the bridge is correctly installed. If not, go back and check your `PATH` variable to be sure it's correct.

While you're at it, you should developer-enable your Android device, too, so it'll work with ADB. Follow the steps given at `http://bit.ly/1a29sal`.

Configuring Qt Creator

Now, it's time to tell Qt Creator about all the stuff you just installed:

1. Start Qt Creator, but don't create a new project.
2. Under the **Tools** menu, choose **Options...** and then **Android**.
3. Fill in the blanks, as the next screenshot shows. They should be:
    1. The path to the SDK directory in the directory where you installed the Android SDK.
    2. The path to where you installed the Android NDK.
    3. Check **Automatically create kits for Android tool chains**.
    4. The path to Ant; either the Ant executable itself on Mac OS X and Linux platforms, or `ant.bat` in the bin directory of the directory where you unpacked Ant.
    5. The directory where you installed the JDK (this may be automatically picked up from your `JAVA_HOME` directory).

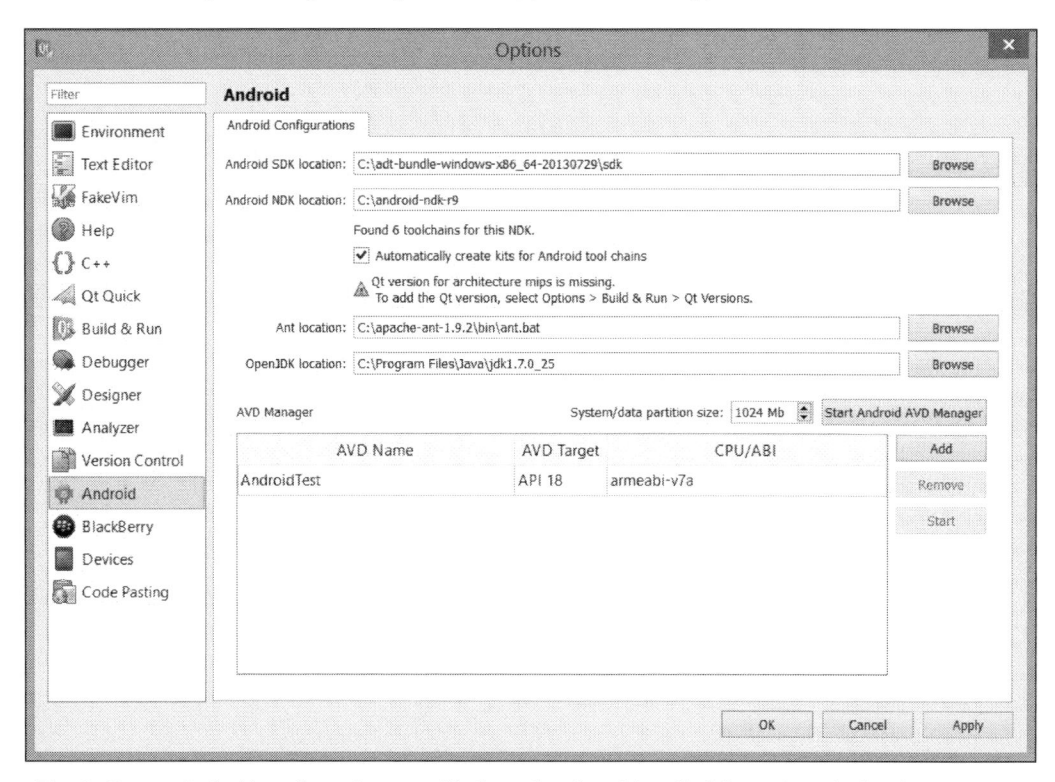

The Qt Creator Android configuration, set with the paths where I installed the various Android components

6. Click on **OK** to close the **Options** window.

You should now be able to create a new Qt GUI or Qt Quick application for Android! Do so, and ensure that Android is a target option in the wizard as the next screenshot shows; be sure to choose at least one ARM target, one x86 target, and one target for your desktop environment:

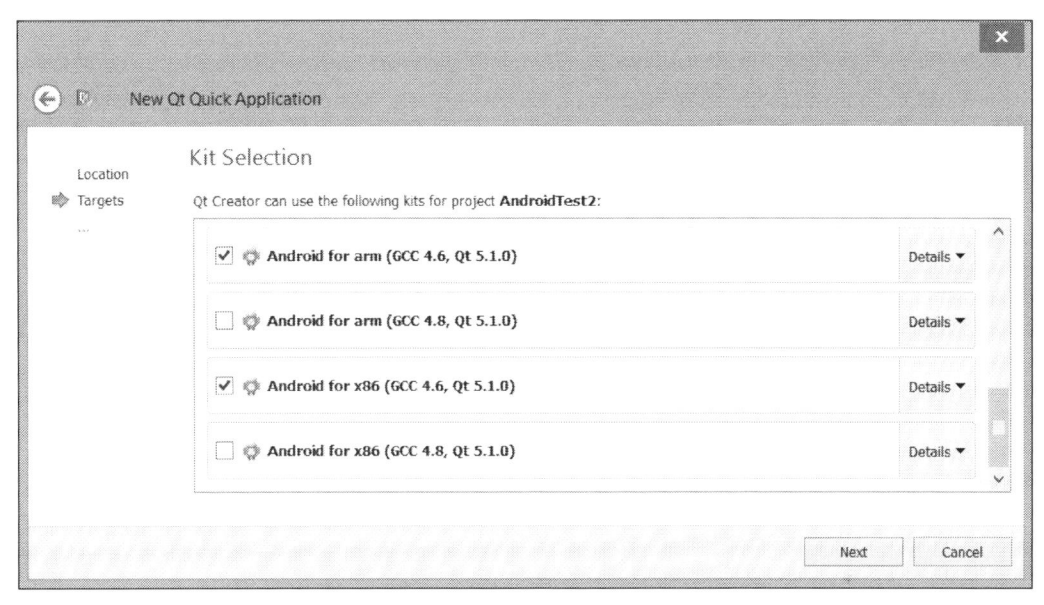

Android targets in the New Qt Quick Application wizard

Building and running your application

Write and build your application normally. A good idea is to first build the Qt Quick "Hello World" application for Android, before you go to town and make a lot of changes, and test the environment by compiling for the device. When you're ready to run on the device:

1. Navigate to **Projects** (on the left) and then choose the **Android for arm** kit's **Run Settings**.
2. Under **Package Configurations**, ensure that the Android SDK level is set to the SDK level of the SDK you installed.
3. Ensure that **Package name** reads something like `org.qtproject.example`, followed by your project name.
4. Connect your Android device to your computer using the USB cable.
5. Choose the **Android for arm** run target, and then click on either **Debug** or **Run** to debug or run your application on the device.

Summary

Qt for Android gives you an excellent leg up on mobile development, but it's not a panacea. If you're planning on targeting mobile devices, you should be sure to have a good understanding of the usage patterns for your application's users, as well as the constraints in CPU, GPU, memory, and network that a mobile application must run under.

Once we understand these, all of our skills with Qt Creator and Qt carry over to the mobile arena. Begin by installing the JDK, Android SDK, Android NDK, and Ant, and then develop applications as usual, compiling for the device and running on the device frequently to iron out any unexpected problems along the way.

In our final chapter, we learn a bunch of odds and ends about Qt Creator and Qt in general that will make software development much easier. Stay tuned!

Qt Tips and Tricks

In the previous chapters, we've discussed what makes Qt Creator a great toolkit for your software development: how to edit, compile, and debug applications; how to profile their execution and memory performance; how to localize them for different regions of the world; and even how to make mobile applications that run on Android phones and tablets. In this chapter, we will discuss a collection of tips and tricks you should know about when using Qt Creator and Qt that will have you writing software like a pro.

Writing console applications with Qt Creator

Remember the "Hello World" application in *Chapter 1*, *Getting Started with Qt Creator*? That was a console application, about as simple a one as you can write. Recapping the code, we created a new Qt console application, and in `main.cpp` we wrote:

```
#include <QCoreApplication>
#include <iostream>

using namespace std;

int main(int argc, char *argv[])
{
    QCoreApplication a(argc, argv);

    cout << "Hello world!";

    return a.exec();
}
```

Any valid C++ is valid in a Qt application, including Standard Template Library (STL) code. This is especially handy if you need to write a small tool in C++, and haven't learned a lot about Qt yet: everything you know about C++ (and even C, if you prefer) is accessible to you in Qt Creator.

Although Qt is most widely known as a GUI toolkit, it's worth mentioning that the `QtCore` library, part of every Qt application including Qt console applications, includes a bevy of utility and template classes, such as:

- Collection classes, including `QList`, `QVector`, `QStack`, and `QQueue` for keeping lists and vectors, and for last-in-first-out and first-in-first-out data storage
- Dictionary classes (otherwise known as hash tables), including `QMap` and `QDict`
- Cross-platform file I/O with `QFile` and `QDirectory`
- Unicode string support with `QString`

Why will you choose Qt's classes over what straight C++ provides you? There are a few reasons:

- **Memory performance**: Unlike STL collections, Qt collections are reference based, and use copy-on-write to save memory. Qt collections typically take less memory than their STL counterparts.
- **Iteration**: Iterating over Qt collections is safe, with guarded access to prevent walking off the end of a collection.
- **Readability**: Using Qt code and libraries throughout an application provides a uniform look and feel that can make the code easier to maintain.
- **Portability**: On some embedded platforms where Qt is available, the STL may not be. (This isn't nearly the problem it was when Qt was first being written, however.)

It's worth noting that Qt's collections are often slightly slower than their STL counterparts: when using a Qt class for data, you're often trading memory performance for speed. In practice, however, this is rarely a problem.

The `QFile` and `QDirectory` classes are worth a special mention, because of one thing: **portability**. Even directory separators are handled in a portable way; directories are always demarcated by a single /, regardless of whether you're running on Mac OS X, Linux, or Windows, making it easy to write your code in a platform-agnostic way and ensure that it runs on all platforms. Under the hood, Qt translates directory strings to use the platform-specific directory separator when accessing files.

Integration with version control systems

Nearly all large projects require some sort of version control to coordinate changes made to the same files by different users, and ensure that changes to a source base occur harmoniously. Even a single developer can benefit by using version control, because version control provides a record of what changed in each file the developer has changed, and provides a valuable history of the project over time. Qt Creator supports the following version control systems:

- Bazaar (supported in Qt Creator in Version 2.2 and beyond)
- CVS
- Git
- Mercurial (supported in Qt Creator in Version 2.0 and beyond)
- Perforce (supporting Perforce Server Version 2006.1 and later)
- Subversion

The first thing you need to do is set up version control software for your project. How to do this depends on the version control system you choose (it may be dictated by your organization, for example, or you may have a personal preference from working on past projects), and how you do this differs from system to system, so we won't go into it here. But, you need to have a repository to store the versions of your source code, and have the appropriate version control software installed on your workstation with the appropriate directories containing the version control binaries in your system's PATH environment variable, so that Qt Creator can find them. It's important that you access the version control commands from your system's shell (such as PowerShell or your local terminal prompt), because Qt Creator accesses them in the same ways.

Once we've done this, we can configure how Qt Creator interacts with version control by selecting **Tools | Options… | Version Control**. There are general configuration options, which apply to whatever version control system you're using, and then specific options for each flavor of version control that Qt supports. The general options are:

- A script that can be run on any submission message to ensure that your message is formatted correctly or contains the right information
- A list of names and aliases for your source code control system
- A list of fields to include in each submission message
- The SSH prompt command used to prompt you for your SSH password when using SSH to access your version control system

Some version control systems, such as Git and Mercurial, support local version control repositories. This is handy if you're flying solo on a development project and just need a place to back up your changes (of course, remember to back up the source code repository directory as well!). If you're using one of these systems, you can use Qt to create the local repository directory directly by navigating to **Tools | Create Repository**, or by navigating to **File | New File or Project** wizard on its last page.

If you install and configure a version control system, the various commands available from that system are added in a submenu to the **Tools** menu of Qt Creator. From there, you can:

- View version control command output by navigating to **Window | Output Panes | Version Control**
- View different output from your version control system, letting you see what's changed in a file you are editing from what's in the repository
- View the change log for a file under version control by choosing **Log** or **Filelog**
- Commit a file's changes to the system by choosing **Commit** or **Submit**
- Revert changes to a file by choosing **Revert**
- Update your working directory with the current contents of the version control system by choosing **Update**
- Access additional per-version-control commands for supporting branches, stashes, and remote repositories that may also be available

If you're just starting out and need to choose a version control system, perhaps the best thing to do is to look at the comparison of various systems on Wikipedia at `http://bit.ly/1aVGEUa` and get familiar with one.

> Personally, I prefer Git for my work, both using local repositories and in-hosted repositories such as GitHub. It's free, fast, has good support for branching, and is well-supported by Qt Creator.

Configuring coding style and coding format options

Readable code is crucial, and Qt Creator's default coding style is one that most people find very readable. However, you may be on a project with different coding guidelines, or you may just find you can't bear a particular facet of how the Qt Creator editor deals with code formatting: maybe it's the positioning of the brackets, or how a `switch` statement gets formatted. Fortunately, Qt Creator is extremely configurable. By navigating to **Tools** | **Options…** | **C++**, you can configure how Qt Creator formats your code, as shown in the following screenshot:

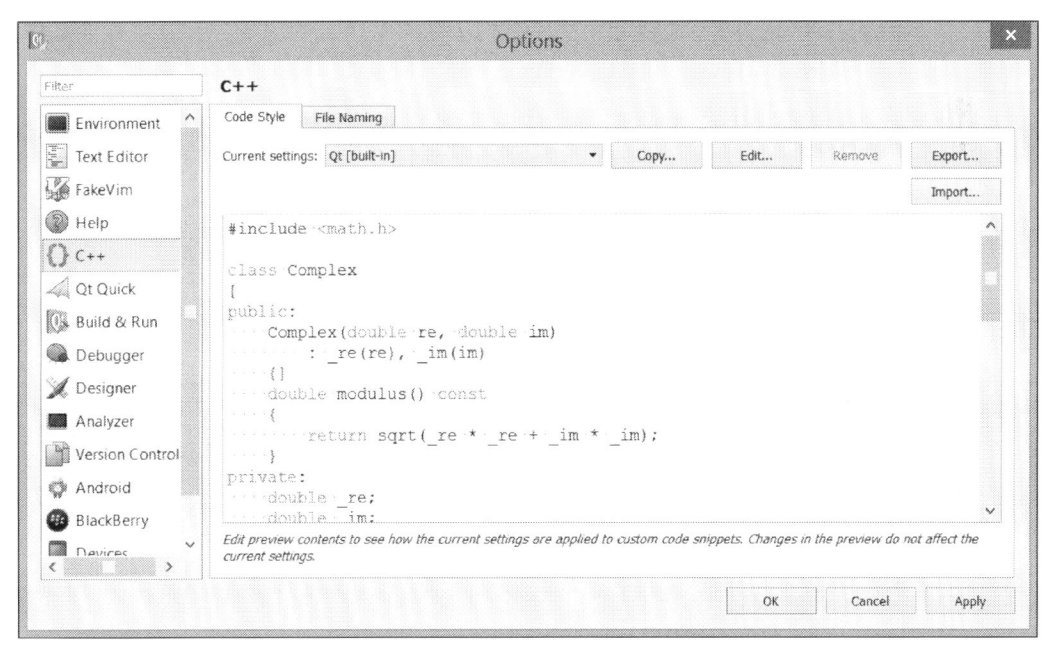

Adjusting code formatting in Qt Creator

The basic dialog lets you pick popular formatting styles, such as Qt's default format, or the format used by most GNU code. You can also click on **Edit...**, which brings up the **Edit Code Style** window, as shown in the next screenshot:

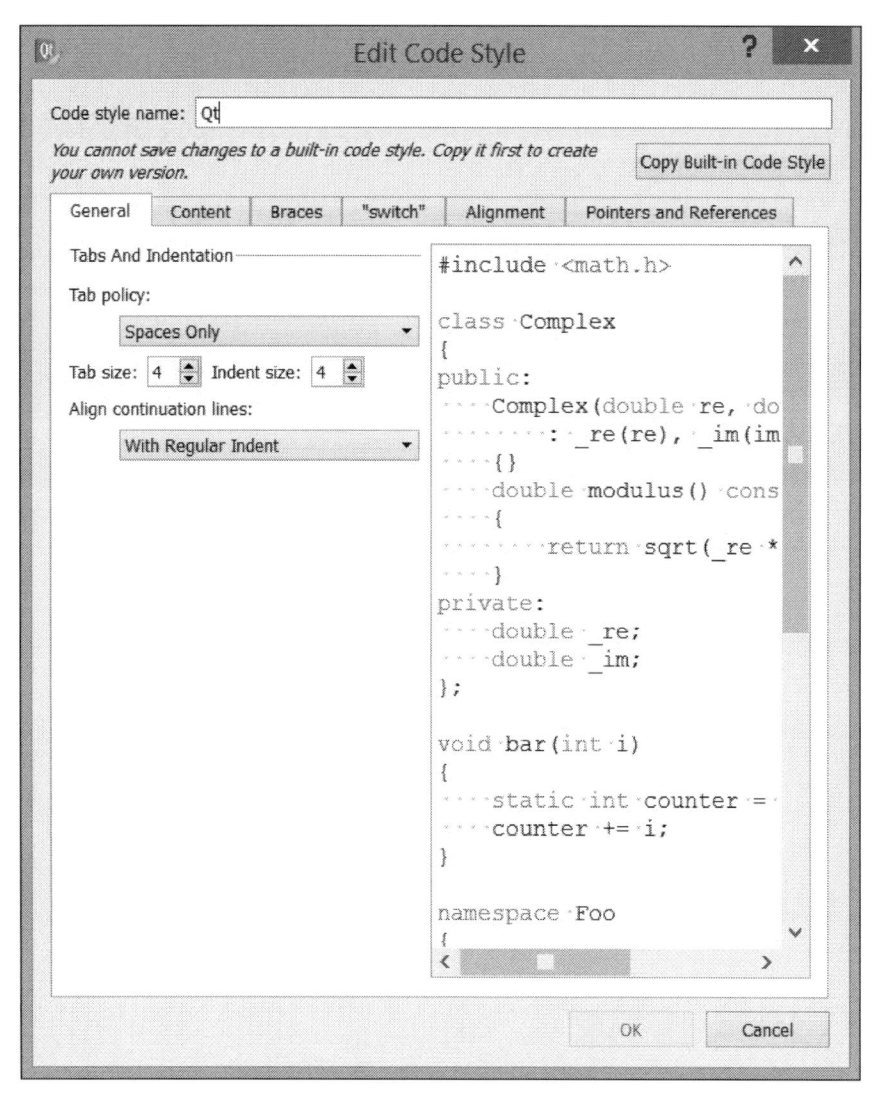

Fine-tuning code formatting in Qt Creator

You'll want to begin by copying a built-in style and editing it to suit your tastes; from the **Edit Code Style** dialog you can select whether tabs are represented as tab characters or spaces or tabs and the number of spaces per tab stop, as well as how line continuations are handled. Each pane lets you adjust specific aspects of code formatting:

- The **Content** pane lets you adjust how class bodies are formatted, including spacing for public, protected, and private declarations
- The **Braces** pane lets you control formatting as it pertains to braces
- The "**switch**" pane lets you control switch and case statement formatting
- The **Alignment** pane lets you control how code is aligned between consecutive lines
- The **Pointer and References** pane lets you control spacing around pointer declarations

It's easy to go crazy with all these options, but I urge you not to: what looks good at first glance is often an unreadable mess when you see it day after day. If you're just getting started with Qt, stick with the default formatting, and remember the old adage *To do no harm*. When it comes to editing existing code—match the formatting that's already there.

Building from the command line

Sometimes, you need to build a project from the command line. Maybe you're working on Linux, and you're just more comfortable there, or you've got a remote session running to your desktop while you're in a meeting. Or maybe, you want to automate builds on a build server, and need to know how Qt does its compilation magic for your builds.

The trick is `qmake`: Qt's meta-make system that manages generating Make files for the compiler toolchain you already have installed. The `qmake` command takes `.pro` files, which you first saw in *Chapter 2, Building Applications with Qt Creator*, and generates the Make or Nmake file necessary for your toolchain to build your application.

First, be sure that you have your compiler and `make` utility in your system path: how you do this varies from development environment to development environment. Next, be sure that you have commands for Qt's build system in your path—a default if you've installed Qt on Linux using the package manager, and easily done by editing your path to include the appropriate `bin` directory from the Qt tools you installed on Mac OS X or Windows.

Next, open up a command window and change to the directory containing your project: your `.pro` file should be at the root of that directory. Type `qmake`, and then either make (if your build system uses `make`), or `nmake` (if you're using a Microsoft Windows toolchain). That's all there is to it!

Setting Qt Quick window display options

Qt Quick is great for building applications for nontraditional computing environments, such as set-top boxes or automotive computers. Often, when working with Qt Quick you'll want an application that doesn't have all the usual windows chrome (such as the close box) around the contents of the window in these settings, because you're trying to present a unified user interface based on your Qt Quick application, rather than the windowing toolkit on the host platform.

You can easily set opacity and windows options (such as whether or not to show a close box) by editing the `main.cpp` file in your Qt Quick project. By default, it looks like this:

```
#include <QtGui/QGuiApplication>
#include "qtquick2applicationviewer.h"

int main(int argc, char *argv[])
{
    QGuiApplication app(argc, argv);

    QtQuick2ApplicationViewer viewer;
    viewer.setMainQmlFile(QStringLiteral
        ("qml/QtTranslucent/main.qml"));
    viewer.showExpanded();

    return app.exec();
}
```

This code creates a Qt Quick application viewer, sets its main QML file (the first one to be loaded) to the indicated file, and then shows it before starting the application's event loop. Fortunately, the `QtQuick2ApplicationViewer` object has a `setFlags` method that lets you pass `Qt::Window` flags to the window it initializes to display your Qt Quick application. These flags include:

- `Qt::FramelessWindowHint`: This indicates that the window should be borderless (works on Linux systems, but not on Windows)
- `Qt::Popup`: This indicates a pop-up window (you can use this on Windows to get a nearly borderless window with a slight drop shadow)
- `Qt::WindowStaysOnTopHint`: This indicates that the window should stay on top of all other windows
- `Qt::WindowStaysOnBottomHint`: This indicates that the window should stay below all other windows
- `Qt::Desktop`: This indicates that the window should run on the desktop

A full list of the flags can be found in the Qt documentation at http://bit.
ly/17NT0sm.

You can also adjust a window's opacity, by using the setOpacity method of
QtQuick2ApplicationViewer.

Say, for example, we want a blue window with no border but a slight drop shadow
at 75 percent opacity to hover over all other windows for my Qt Quick application.
We'd change the QML to read:

```
import QtQuick 2.0

Rectangle {
    width: 360
    height: 360
    color: "blue"
    Text {
        text: qsTr("Hello World")
        anchors.centerIn: parent
        font.pointSize: 18
    }
    MouseArea {
        anchors.fill: parent
        onClicked: {
            Qt.quit();
        }
    }
}
```

Note the color: blue declaration for our top-level rectangle. Next, we'd modify
main.cpp to read:

```
#include <QtGui/QGuiApplication>
#include "qtquick2applicationviewer.h"

int main(int argc, char *argv[])
{
    QGuiApplication app(argc, argv);

    QtQuick2ApplicationViewer viewer;
    viewer.setOpacity(0.75);
    viewer.setFlags(Qt::Popup | Qt::WindowStaysOnTopHint);
    viewer.setMainQmlFile(QStringLiteral("qml/QtTranslucent/main.qml"));
    viewer.showExpanded();

    return app.exec();
}
```

Qt Tips and Tricks

The key lines here come just before `viewer.setMainQmlFile`: the `setOpacity` method sets the main window's opacity, and the `setFlags` method sets the flags for the main window to be a pop up that will be on top of all other windows. By running the application, we can see something like the following screenshot:

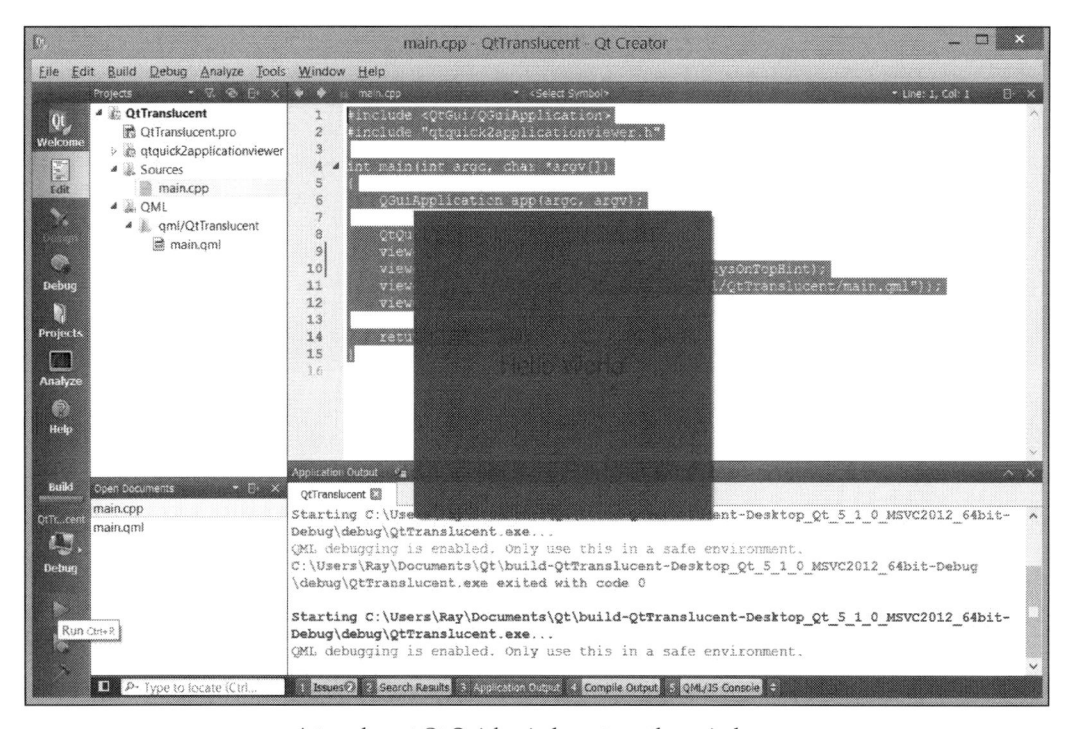

A translucent Qt Quick window atop other windows

You can use this trick to come up with a variety of effects for how your Qt Quick application is displayed.

Learning more about Qt

In the earlier chapters, I pointed you to the **Help** panel of Qt Creator, as well as the editor's facility for autocompletion of class members when editing code. The Qt Creator's **Help** view is really a subview into Qt Assistant, the full documentation for all of Qt. Much of this documentation is also on the Web, but it's much faster to access locally. We start Qt Assistant from the Qt SDK (either from the command line with `qtassistant` or by finding it in the installed list of applications), and we can see something like the following screenshot:

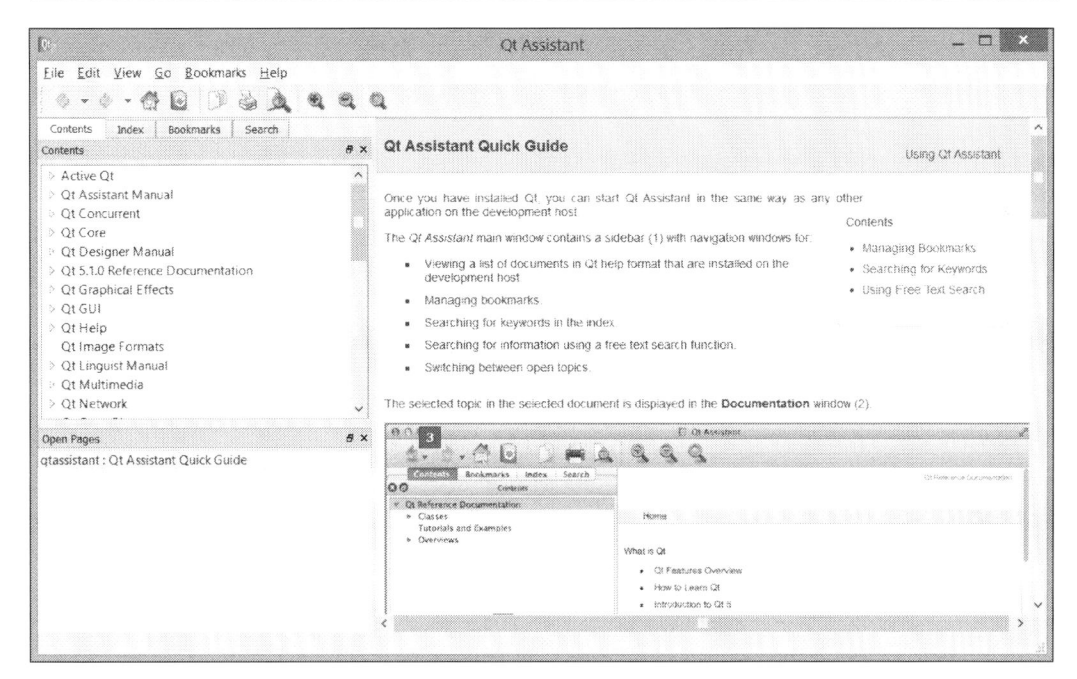

Qt Assistant

Qt Assistant is the definitive place to learn about Qt. In the left column you see a table of contents; the best place to start is with Qt Core, and then either Qt GUI or Qt Quick depending on whether you want to write GUI or Qt Quick applications. The main view on the right is just like a browser window, complete with hyperlinks to related sections.

Also inside Qt Assistant, you can add bookmarks to frequently accessed pages, see an index of all terms in the documentation, and quickly search for terms using the search tab in the left-hand column. It's an invaluable resource, and as easy to use as an e-book.

Finally, if you prefer the Web for learning about things, don't forget Qt's extensive online documentation, available at `http://bit.ly/15F110k`.

Summary

Qt and Qt Creator provide a great environment for your application development, whether you're writing console, GUI, or Qt Quick applications. You can mix and match standard C++ code with Qt, letting you make the most of your existing skills. When doing so, you can add in things such as version control and command-line builds to your tools, giving you the ability to work in large teams and perform unattended builds of large projects using Qt. Qt also has a great documentation both bundled with Qt Creator and on the Web. With what you've learned in this book and what's available, the sky's the limit for your application development goals!

Index

A

About button 54, 56
aboutButton button 53
Add New option 29
Alignment pane 111
Analyze menu 86
Android
  Qt Creator, setting up for 98-103
Android for arm run target 103
Android SDK installation
  finishing 100, 101
Ant
  downloading 99
application
  building 103
  creating, Qt Designer used 49-55
  debugging 42, 43
  dialogs, initiating in 55-59
  forms, initiating in 55-59
  localizing 75, 76
  localizing, with Qt Linguist 77-79
  message boxes, initiating in 55-59
  running 42, 43, 103
arguments function 63
arguments method 62
auto-suggest 24

B

binding 65
Braces pane 111
breakpoint
  about 33
  controlling 36, 37
  setting 33-35

Build directory path 24
Build menu 24
Build & Run options 41
Build & Run settings 41
Build Settings editor 41
buttonText.text property 69

C

CalculatorLogic object 65
calculator main view 70-72
call stack
  examining 39, 40
CDB pane 31
Code Style options 41
Code Style panel 42
coding format options
  configuring 109-111
coding style
  configuring 109-111
command line
  building from 111
command-line debugger
  installing 31-33
CONFIG variable 26
console applications
  writing, Qt creator used 105, 106
Content pane 111
Continue button 38
Counter class 46-48
Counter object 49
currencies
  localizing 81

D

date formatting 81
dates
  localizing 81
Debug button 33
Debug menu 35
Debug view 33
delay property 85
Dependencies panel 42
DEPENDPATH variable 30
Dialog class 59
dialogs
  initiating, in application 55-59
divideButton button 52
divideClicked method 63

E

Edit Code Style dialog 110
Edit Code Style window 110
Editor options 41
Editor panel 42
emit keyword 70
environment variables
  setting up 99, 100
Events view 88
exec method 57
Expression Evaluator 37

F

factorial function 21-24, 34, 40
File menu 27, 67
File | New File or Project wizard 108
forms
  initiating, in application 55-59
Forms folder 51

H

Handling Signal row 87
HEADERS variable 26
height property 65

Hello World application
about 10, 11
compiling 11
running 11
with Qt GUI library 12-15
with Qt Quick 16-19
Help panel 114
HTTP 96
Hypertext Transfer Protocol. *See* HTTP

I

INCLUDEPATH variable 30
INSTALLS variable 26
Interrupt button 39

J

Java Development Kit. *See* JDK
JAVA_HOME variable 99, 100
JavaScript view 87, 88
JDK
  about 99
  downloading 99

L

Label widget 54
leakPressed method 90
LIBS variable 27
Line Edit widgets 51
localization
  about 75
  strings, marking for 76, 77
localized strings
  including, in application 80
Long Term Evolution (LTE) 96
lrelease command 75, 76
lupdate command 75, 76

M

main function 40
MainWindow class 58-61, 89, 90
MainWindow constructor 57, 90
MathFunctions class 22, 24

MathFunctions directory 30
MathFunctions library 27, 28, 42
MathFunctionsTest console
      application 27, 30
memory
  examining 37-39
memory leaks
  finding, Valgrind used 88, 89
message boxes
  initiating, in application 55-59
minusButton button 52
minusClicked method 63
mobile application
  performance enhancing, steps 95
mobile application development
  about 93, 94
  computational resources 95
  limited attention, consequences 94
  network resources 96
  storage resources 96
  testing 98
  UI, porting 97
  user attention 94
mouseArea.pressed property 69

N

Native Development Kit. *See* NDK
NDK
  about 99
  downloading 99
New File wizard 58
Noun Project
  URL 54
number method 60

O

onClicked handler 87, 88
on_pushButton_clicked method 15
operation buttons 72
operation property 69
Options dialog 42
Options window 103

P

Package Configurations 103
parseFloat function 72
PATH variable 100
plusButton button 52
Pointer and References pane 111
portability 106
project
  building 41, 42
Project Management window 23
Projects button 24, 41
Projects pane 23
PropertyChange event 69
Publish option 25
Push Button widgets 51

Q

QCoreApplication task 11
qDebug() function 28
QDict class 106
QDirectory class 106
QFile class 106
QList class 106
QLocale::LongFormat 81
QLocale::NarrowFormat 81
QLocale::ShortFormat 81
QMainWindow class 61
QMap class 106
QMessageBox class 57
QMessageBox object 57
QML 45, 73
QML performance analyzer
  about 83, 84
    QtSlowButton performance,
      analyzing 84-87
QML Profiler 86
  tabs 86
QML Profiler tabs
  events 86
  JavaScript 86
  timeline 86
QML syntax
  code interlude 63-66

QNetworkAccessManager class 96
QObject::connect method 48
QPainter object 64
QPair template 61
QPushButton button 48
QPushButton constructor 49
QPushButton object 49
QQueue class 106
QSharedPointer class 88
QStack class 106
qsTr function 76, 77
Qt 7, 114, 115
Qt classes features
  iteration 106
  memory performance 106
  portability 106
  readability 106
QtCore library 106
Qt Creator
  about 7
  configuring 102, 103
  debugging 31-33
  downloading 7-9
  Hello World application 10, 11
  sample library, creating 21-24
  screen 10
  setting up, for Android 98-103
  URL, for free noncommercial version 8
  used, for console applications writing 105, 106
Qt Creator debugging
  breakpoints, controlling 36, 37
  breakpoints, setting 33-35
  call stack, examining 39, 40
  memory, examining 37-39
  variables, examining 37-39
Qt Creator for Android
  all pieces, downloading 99
  application, building 103
  application, running 103
  environment variables, setting up 99, 100
  Qt Creator, configuring 102, 103
  SDK installation, finishing 100, 101
Qt Creator sample library
  about 21
  creating 22-24
  linking against 27-30

Qt Designer
  application resources, using 54
  forms, creating in 49-55
  main form, creating in 50-54
  Qt Quick applications, creating in 66-73
  used, for creating application 49-55
Qt Designer Form Class 58
Qt framework key concepts
  signals 49
Qt framework, key concepts
  signals 46-49
  slots 46-49
Qt GUI application logic
  wiring 59-63
Qt GUI library
  Hello World application 12-15
Qt GUI widgets 63
QtLeakyButton
  memory leaks, finding with Valgrind 89-92
Qt Linguist
  about 75
  used, for localizing application 77-79
Qt Meta-object Language. *See* QML
Qt project pane 41, 42
Qt Quick
  about 16, 73
  applications, creating in Qt Designer 66-73
  code interlude 63-66
  Hello World application 16-19
  Qt::Window flags 112
  window display options, setting 112-114
QtQuick2ApplicationViewer object 112
Qt Quick applications
  calculator main view 70-73
  creating in Qt Designer 66, 67
  reusable button, creating 67-70
QtSlowButton
  performance, analyzing 84-88
QT variable 26
Qt::Window flags
  Qt::Desktop 112
  Qt::FramelessWindowHint 112
  Qt::Popup 112
  Qt::WindowStaysOnBottomHint 112
  Qt::WindowStaysOnTopHint 112
QVector class 106

R

ResultDialog class 58
ResultDialog implementation 59
ResultDialog object 62, 63
result field 59
results dialog 58
reusable button
　creating 67-69
Row item 72
Run button 53

S

SDK
　about 99
　downloading 99
Select Required Modules window 22
setFlags method 112
setOpacity method 113, 114
setupUi function 56
setupUi method 59
signal keyword 70
SIGNAL macro 49
signals 46
SLOT macro 49
software development 76
Software Development Kit. *See* SDK
SOURCES variable 26
Standard Template Library 11
state property 69
strings
　marking, for localization 76, 77
sudo apt-get install qtcreator command 8

T

TARGET variable 26
TEMPLATE variable 26
testing 98
Text Editor option 42
TextInput field 72
text property 52
timesButton button 52
timesClicked method 63

toFloat method 62
Tool Button widget 53
Tools menu 31, 42, 102
toString method 81
tr function 76

U

Ui:Dialog class 59
ui field 56
Ui::MainWindow class 56

V

Valgrind
　used, for memory leaks finding 88, 89
　used, for QtLeakyButton memory leaks
　　finding 89-92
variables
　examining 37-39
version control systems
　general configuration options 107
　integrating with 107, 108
Vertical Spacer 53

W

when clause 69
width property 65
Windows Firewall dialog 86

X

x property 65

Y

y property 65

Thank you for buying
Application Development with Qt Creator

About Packt Publishing

Packt, pronounced 'packed', published its first book "*Mastering phpMyAdmin for Effective MySQL Management*" in April 2004 and subsequently continued to specialize in publishing highly focused books on specific technologies and solutions.

Our books and publications share the experiences of your fellow IT professionals in adapting and customizing today's systems, applications, and frameworks. Our solution based books give you the knowledge and power to customize the software and technologies you're using to get the job done. Packt books are more specific and less general than the IT books you have seen in the past. Our unique business model allows us to bring you more focused information, giving you more of what you need to know, and less of what you don't.

Packt is a modern, yet unique publishing company, which focuses on producing quality, cutting-edge books for communities of developers, administrators, and newbies alike. For more information, please visit our website: www.packtpub.com.

About Packt Open Source

In 2010, Packt launched two new brands, Packt Open Source and Packt Enterprise, in order to continue its focus on specialization. This book is part of the Packt Open Source brand, home to books published on software built around Open Source licenses, and offering information to anybody from advanced developers to budding web designers. The Open Source brand also runs Packt's Open Source Royalty Scheme, by which Packt gives a royalty to each Open Source project about whose software a book is sold.

Writing for Packt

We welcome all inquiries from people who are interested in authoring. Book proposals should be sent to author@packtpub.com. If your book idea is still at an early stage and you would like to discuss it first before writing a formal book proposal, contact us; one of our commissioning editors will get in touch with you.

We're not just looking for published authors; if you have strong technical skills but no writing experience, our experienced editors can help you develop a writing career, or simply get some additional reward for your expertise.

PACKT PUBLISHING
open source
community experience distilled

PhoneGap 2.x Mobile Application Development Hotshot

ISBN: 978-1-849519-40-3　　　Paperback: 388 pages

Create exciting apps for mobile devices using PhoneGap

1. Ten apps included to help you get started on your very own exciting mobile app
2. These apps include working with localization, social networks, geolocation, as well as the camera, audio, video, plugins, and more
3. Apps cover the spectrum from productivity apps, educational apps, all the way to entertainment and games

Boost C++ Application Development Cookbook

ISBN: 978-1-849514-88-0　　　Paperback: 348 pages

Over 80 practical, task-based recipes to create applications using Boost libraries

1. Explores how to write a program once and then use it on Linux, Windows, Mac OS, and Android operating systems
2. Includes everyday use recipes for multithreading, networking, metaprogramming, and generic programming from a Boost library developer
3. Take advantage of the real power of Boost and C++ to get a good grounding in using it in any project

Please check **www.PacktPub.com** for information on our titles

Express Web Application Development

ISBN: 978-1-849696-54-8　　　Paperback: 236 pages

Learn how to develop web applications with the Express framework from scratch

1. Exploring all aspects of web development using the Express framework
2. Starts with the essentials
3. Expert tips and advice covering all Express topics

Android Studio Application Development

ISBN: 978-1-783285-27-3　　　Paperback: 110 pages

Create visually appealing applications using the new IntelliJ IDE Android Studio

1. Familiarize yourself with Android Studio IDE
2. Enhance the user interface for your app using the graphical editor feature
3. Explore the various features involved in developing an android app and implement them

Please check **www.PacktPub.com** for information on our titles